D1097438

TWELVESWEATERS
ONE WAY

Knitting
Cuff to Cuff

To Arthur for his constant support and encouragement in everything I do.

Creative Publishing international

©2007 Creative Publishing international, Inc.
18705 Lake Drive East
Chanhassen, Minnesota 55317
1-800-328-3895
www.creativepub.com

Library of Congress Cataloging-in-Publication Data
Guagliumi, Susan,
    Knitting cuff to cuff : a dozen designs for sideways-knit garments / Susan Guagliumi.
        p.   cm. — (Twelve sweaters one way)
    ISBN 1-58923-290-9 (pbk.)
    1. Knitting—Patterns. 2. Sweaters. I. Title. II. Series.

TT825.G78 2007
746.43'20432—dc22
                                      2006026617
                                              CIP

ISBN-13: 978-1-58923-290-7
ISBN-10: 1-58923-290-9

Design: Judy Morgan
Page layout: *tabula rasa* graphic design
Photographs: Robert Lisak
Illustrations: Heather Lambert
Schematics: Susan Guagliumi
Painting, page 79: Arthur Guagliumi

Models:
Amy Cannarella Blanco: pages 43, 69
Adam Clemens: page 33
Olivia Cresser: pages 63, 83
Tara DellaCamera: pages 37, 56, 79
Linda Ross Edwards: pages 29, 47
Maliya Ellis: page 51
Ben Guagliumi: pages 33, 72

Printed in Singapore

10 9 8 7 6 5 4 3 2 1

TWELVE SWEATERS
ONE WAY

Knitting
Cuff to Cuff

A DOZEN
DESIGNS FOR
SIDEWAYS-KNIT
GARMENTS

Susan Guagliumi

**Creative Publishing
international**

Chanhassen, MN

contents

CHAPTER ONE

Knitting Cuff to Cuff

Knitting sweaters sideways—or from cuff to cuff—is a fun and versatile alternative to more traditional knitting methods. The garments are knitted just as the name implies. Instead of knitting a sweater along its length—from bottom to top or top to bottom—you knit the garment across its width, from cuff to cuff. The stitches themselves lie horizontally, rather than vertically, within the garment.

Why Knit Sideways?

Cuff-to-cuff knitting has several distinct advantages over the traditional methods, and it also provides the knitter with a new range of design possibilities. Each of the twelve sweaters in this book has the same simple cuff-to-cuff garment as its foundation—but each also showcases one or more unique design features and variations. By working with the basic cuff-to-cuff shape as your canvas, you can vary textures, embellishments, and finishing details to produce a dozen—or more—classic and creative designs.

Color and Stitch Work

Variegated or space-dyed yarns are notorious for creating unfortunate blobs of color when knitted conventionally—bottom to top. The width of the garment affects the runs or repeats of the yarn's color. When the garment width changes at the armholes or when each side of a neckline is shaped separately, the color is concentrated in smaller areas, and so the color effect is often very different from the rest of the sweater.

Knitting cuff to cuff does not totally eliminate this color-pooling effect, but it does minimize it, producing vertical stripes that blend more subtly. Although color patterning runs vertically across the width of a sweater, cables and other stitch work change direction. Instead of reading vertically, as they do in traditional construction, they instead become horizontal elements, adding variety and interest to the finished garment.

Construction and Finishing

Knitting cuff to cuff also affects the way in which garments are constructed and finished. The sweater's sleeves and body are knit all in one piece, so there are fewer seams in the garment, which gives the sweater a smoother surface and a more contoured fit.

Instead of knitting bands and ribs while knitting each section of a garment, as is traditionally done, the bands and ribs are picked up and knitted onto the lower edge of the garment after all the body pieces are knit. In cuff-to-cuff knitting, the front edges of cardigans, for example, do not have selvage edges. Instead, they have live stitches or bound-off or cast-on edges that you can pick up or embellish to finish.

The Twelve Variations

This book presents twelve variations on one simple cuff-to-cuff shape. I've provided a materials list, a schematic drawing of the garment's silhouette, a stitch chart for the particular surface texture or fabric patterning, and step-by-step knitting instructions for each design.

Most of the pullover sweaters are worked in one piece and require seams only on the sides and at the underarms. These sweaters have typical shaping for sleeves and necklines. The basic cuff-to-cuff sweater, on which all the others are based, is presented as the Crayon Stripes pullover on pages 28–31. I've discussed the strategy and techniques for making this first sweater in great detail to introduce you to the basic concepts and skills you'll need to make all the sweaters in the book.

As I introduce design variations on the basic cuff-to-cuff garment, I'll also discuss the knitting skills you'll need to create those variations. For example, I worked short rows to add fullness and flare to Flirt (page 82), and I have

THE TWELVE SWEATER VARIATONS

Sweater	Stitch Pattern	Gauge	Style	Bands	Details
Crayon Stripes	Stockinette	5	Women's pullover	K1p1 rib	Rolled edges
Weekend Woodsman	Knit/purl texture stitch	5	Men's pullover	K2p2 rib	"Gourmet" bind-off method
Chiquita Jacketta	Stockinette and seed stitch	2.25	Women's cardigan	Corrugated stockinette	Shaped collar, patch pockets, mixed gauges
Summer Twist	Twisted stitches	5.25	Women's short-sleeved pullover	Garter stitch	Garter stitch ties and bands
Jewels	Garter stitch with slides	4.5	Women's shrug	Crochet	Extended front ties, three yarns
Classic Stripes	Garter stitch	5	Children's pullover	None	Decorative hemline
Autumn Leaves	Gathered stitch pattern	4	Women's cardigan	Striped k2p2 rib	Buttonholes, optional shawl collar
Corn and Cables	Popcorns, cables, and twisted stitches	6	Women's pullover	Self-rolled edge and I-cord	Texture stitches
Fan Dancer	Fan stitch	5.25	Women's pullover	I-cord	Shaped front, combined seaming, attached I-cord edging, asymmetrical construction
Boys' Club	6 x 6 rib	5	Boys' boatneck pullover	Turned hem	Stripes made with carried and changed yarns, tails worked in while knitting
Luscious	Stockinette and seed stitch	4.5	Women's pullover	Seed stitch	Funnel neck, side slits, reversed sleeve seams
Flirt	Stockinette	4	Women's gored pullover	Crochet	Short-rowed gores, asymmetrical neckline

included detailed instructions for knitting short rows in that section. For some patterns, I offer alternative construction methods and design details, so choose those that most appeal to you.

The Five Steps

Each of the sweaters has stitch patterning, garment features, and finishing details that ultimately make it unique—but each of the sweaters is knitted with the same basic five steps. The schematic for the basic cuff-to-cuff garment, shown on the facing page, is coded with numerals 1 to 5 to correspond to each of the five steps.

The detailed schematic that accompanies each individual set of sweater instructions indicates exactly how long or how many stitches to knit for each section of the garment. Refer to the schematic and the step-by-step written instructions as you work through each design.

Step 1: Knitting the Right Sleeve

The first step is to cast on the number of stitches required for the right sleeve. You then knit the sleeve, increasing as the pattern specifies for your size. You may begin some sleeves with a band. For others, you will apply knitted or crocheted bands as part of the finishing.

You have two choices when you cast on the sleeve: regardless of how an individual pattern is worded, you can cast on with either the main yarn or with scrap yarn. Cast on with scrap yarn if you need "live" stitches—stitches that you can continue to work— at the cuff of the sleeve in order to add a decorative edge treatment when you've finished knitting the garment.

Because you begin your knitting with one sleeve and end with the other, the edges will differ if you work conventional cast-on and bind-off

methods—which is why I prefer to begin and end with scrap knitting (pages 19–20). With scrap knitting, both sleeves are bound off, and I can create the finished edge I want. (Before you cast on, read through to the end of the pattern to determine whether or not your cast-on method will affect the finishing instructions.)

Step 2: Knitting to the Neckline

When you finish knitting the first sleeve, you need to cast on additional stitches on either side of the sleeve to create the fabric that will make up the front and back sections of the garment.

These two cast-on edges ultimately become the side seam—so your method of casting on will affect the final seaming method and appearance. You can use the main yarn to cast on the required number of stitches and then continue knitting the body of the sweater. Or, you can use a scrap yarn cast-on to retain live stitches for invisible seaming, knit a couple of rows with scrap, and then change to the main yarn.

Each row is worked back and forth from the lower edge of the front to the lower edge of the back, until the shoulder measures the necessary length from the top of the sleeve to the beginning of the neck shaping.

Step 3: Shaping the Front Neckline

You can hold the back stitches at one end of the needle while the front neckline is being shaped. Or you can transfer the back stitches to a stitch holder until you need to knit them. The front neckline is shaped according to the pattern instructions—usually by decreasing stitches at the right edge of the neckline, working some rows without further shaping, then increasing stitches for the left side of the neckline. After you shape the neckline, you place all the front stitches on a stitch holder. (Experienced knitters may prefer to work both the front and back necklines at the same time, using two balls of yarn.)

Step 4: Knitting the Back and the Left Shoulder

Next you knit the back neckline. If you put the back stitches on a stitch holder to knit the front neckline, return them to the needle. Now knit the back neckline, shaping or not, as specified in the pattern. When you finish the back neckline, the front and back of the garment should measure the same from the body's cast-on edges. Return the front stitches to the needle and work across all the front and back garment stitches to complete the left shoulder.

Step 5: Knitting the Left Sleeve

To knit the left sleeve, you need to bind off (or scrap off)—at the end of each needle—the same number of body stitches that were cast on in Step 2. Leave enough stitches at the center of the needle for the top of the sleeve.

If you cast on with the main yarn in Step 2, simply bind off the specified number of stitches at the beginning of the next two rows. The resulting side seams will incorporate cast-on and bound-off edges.

If you chose to cast on with scrap yarn—also called an open cast-on—in Step 2, knit a couple of rows with scrap yarn at one end of the needle. Then bind off these stitches and repeat for the stitches at the other end of the needle. The sleeve is knit on the remaining stitches, decreasing as needed for shaping until the sleeve length matches the right sleeve. Then bind off or scrap off the remaining stitches.

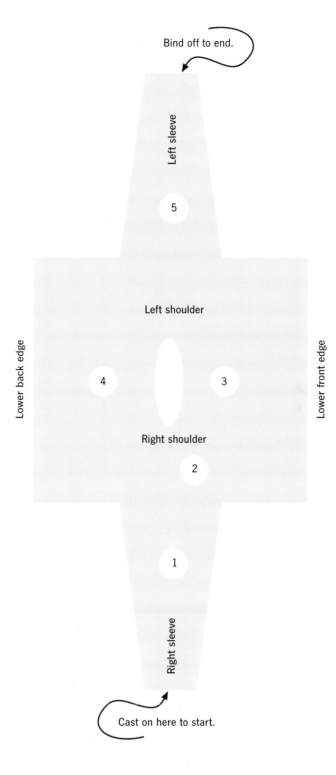

Schematic for basic cuff-to-cuff garment

Before You Begin

Some processes are essential to all knitting patterns, regardless of the direction in which you knit the pieces. For example, you always need to knit a swatch to check your gauge. You must also be able to follow the pattern directions for shaping, stitch work, and other construction details.

Considering Yarn

Gauge indicates the number of stitches produced by a particular combination of yarn and needle size. Gauge is measured by the number of stitches and rows per inch or per centimeter. Each of the sweater patterns in this book specifies the required gauge and provides information on the yarn used to knit the model garment that is featured in the project photograph.

It is always best to use the yarn that a sweater pattern calls for, but if that yarn is not available, you can usually substitute a yarn that has the same recommended gauge and yardage. This information is indicated by the yarn manufacturer as the number of yards/meters per 1.75 ounce/50 gram ball of yarn. The yardage provides a good starting point, but by no means

does it guarantee that the substitute yarn will work up at the same gauge. Gauge depends on other factors, including how you knit, so be sure to check the gauge of your knitted swatch.

The yarn for the body of the sweater is considered the "main yarn," abbreviated MC (main color), but there may also be several contrasting colors in your sweater design. The colored yarns are designated as CC1 (contrast color 1), CC2, and so forth.

If you begin and end sections of your knitting with scrap knitting, choose a yarn that is about the same general thickness as your main yarn, but choose a sharply contrasting color so that you will be able to see the stitches you are trying to pick up. Scrap yarn should always be a smooth cotton or acrylic so it will not leave behind any telltale fuzz when you remove the scrap knitting from the garment stitches.

Check the ball band or skein label for washing directions and always test your swatch for washability. You should also see how the swatch holds up to steaming. Some synthetics should not be steamed at all. If exposed to heat, they are essentially "killed," which means they lose elasticity, sag, and flatten—they can even melt if the heat is a tad too hot.

The All-Important Swatch

Knitting is based on gauge, which indicates how many stitches and rows form an inch of fabric. The yarn itself is a large factor in determining gauge, but the way the designer uses the yarn and the characteristics of the specific stitch work greatly affect the final gauge.

If you are designing your own knits, there really isn't a wrong gauge. If you like the way the fabric feels, looks, and drapes, the gauge is right. When you are working with another person's designs, however, you have to match the recommended gauge in order for the sweater to knit to size—and to determine the gauge, you have to knit at least one swatch. Think of your swatch as an insurance policy. With just a small investment of time and materials, you are guaranteeing that the sweater fits when all your knitting is done.

For conventionally knitted sweaters, the number of stitches determines the width of a piece, and the number of rows determines the length. In cuff-to-cuff knitting, the relationships are reversed: the number of stitches determines the length of the garment; the number of rows determines the width.

Most patterns define their gauge as the number of stitches and rows in a 4" (10 cm) swatch. It's best to cast on as many stitches as the gauge swatch requires and to knit the same number of rows—with the hope of knitting a perfect 4" (10 cm) square. Patterns will usually instruct you to knit the swatch in the same stitch you'll use for the sweater.

If the finished swatch does in fact measure 4" (10 cm), you can start knitting. If not, you'll need to switch to a different needle size until it does. If your swatch measures more then 4" (10 cm), use a smaller needle to get more stitches to the inch or centimeter. If your swatch measures less than 4" (10 cm), work with a larger needle to get fewer stitches to the inch or centimeter.

It is always tempting to stretch the swatch or scrunch it a little so that it measures the required 4" (10 cm), but there really isn't any such thing as "close enough" when it comes to matching gauge. For example, if the gauge indicates 22 stitches in a 4" swatch (5.5 stitches per inch [2.5 cm]), after knitting 110 stitches the fabric should measure 20" (51 cm) wide. If your swatch doesn't *actually* measure 4" (10 cm), however, look what happens to those 110 stitches:

If your swatch measures	110 stitches will measure
4.5" (11.5 cm)	22.5" (57 cm)
4.25" (11 cm)	21.25" (54 cm)
4" (10 cm)	20" (51 cm)
3.75" (9.5 cm)	18.75" (47.5 cm)
3.5" (9 cm)	17.5" (44.5 cm)

In a conventionally knitted sweater, the body could be as much as 5" (13 cm) too large or small once the error is repeated in the front and the back. With a cuff-to-cuff sweater, the error would be obvious in the garment length. So remember, even slight discrepancies in gauge can add up to a sweater that just doesn't fit!

Row gauge is also important, especially when knitting a cuff-to-cuff sweater. Row gauge not only affects the length of the sleeves (as it would for a conventionally knitted sweater), it also affects the width of the body. It is always a good idea to recheck your gauge every so often as you knit.

Needles and Notions

Although straight needles will work just fine for knitting the sleeves, chances are they won't be long enough to hold all the body stitches. I suggest you work with circular 29" (approximately 80 cm) needles for the front/back sections and 24" (approximately 60 cm) needles for the sleeves. Neckbands will require 16" (approximately 40 cm) circulars or double-pointed needles.

Be aware that some sweaters can get fairly weighty as you progress through the body and second sleeve. You may find one style of needle easier to handle than another, so choose whichever works best for you. There will likely be a difference in the gauge each type of needle produces—especially when working with heavy yarns. So, don't switch back and forth between straights and circulars in the same garment unless you have swatched with both and know that your gauge is consistent.

Most knitting needle companies make stitch holders, which come in several sizes and shapes. I have some that look like giant safety pins, without the loop at the end, that stay securely closed. I also like the ones that look like double-pointed needles, with two end caps connected by a spring, because they allow you to remove stitches from either end.

Instead of a stitch holder, you can work with a second circular needle to hold the back garment stitches while you are knitting the front. Place tip protectors or rubber bands on the ends of the needle to keep the stitches from slipping off.

Here are a few of the notions you might need. You won't need all of them for every sweater style, so check the materials list for each pattern for specific suggestions. Many of these items are things you probably already have in your knitting bag.

- **stitch markers**
- **stitch holders**
- **tape measure**
- **cable needle**
- **crochet hook**
- **Addi Turbo Cro-Needle**
- **tapestry needle**
- **yellow highlighter**

You'll also need these supplies when it comes time to block the finished garment:

- **large-head pins**
- **a good steam iron**
- **padded surface that can be pinned into**
- **blocking wires (nice to have, but not necessary)**

Tools pictured at left include assorted needles, the Addi Turbo Cro-Needle (upper left), and stitch holders.

Every pattern suggests a needle size for knitting to gauge, but you may actually have to work with a larger or smaller needle to get the row and stitch gauge you need. Everyone's knitting tension is different, and sometimes a person's tension can change from day to day.

Your needles can also affect the knitting tension—both because of the material type and because needle sizes often differ slightly from one brand to the next. Circular needles can also create a different tension than straights.

Wood and bamboo needles keep stitches from slipping too easily (a good thing for beginners!) so the knitting gauge tends to be a little tighter with these needles. Plastic, resin, and coated-metal needles offer a little more slip. The shiny metal needles preferred by experienced knitters are slick and fast. Sometimes, you can fine-tune your gauge just by switching from a wooden needle to a metal one of the same size.

When you have finished knitting your swatch, bind it off. Then, before you measure for gauge, wash or steam the swatch, just as you would the finished sweater. Always check yarn labels for specific washing instructions, but most wools and blends can be washed or at least steamed by holding the iron a few inches above them.

Many yarns bloom, shrink, or stretch when they are washed. If you do not account for this before you settle on your gauge, you will spend a lot of time knitting a sweater that fits just fine— until the first time it is washed. This step is especially important for cotton yarns. When I work with cotton, I always knit a couple of gauge swatches, including at least one that looks looser than it should. Then I hand-wash and machine-dry the swatches—exactly as I would my cotton sweater—before I measure for gauge. I select the swatch that has the correct gauge after it's been washed and dried.

Pattern Instructions

Most patterns are written for several sizes. Throughout the instructions, the smallest size is listed first and the increasingly larger sizes follow in parentheses. It's sometimes easy to be confused by all the numbers, so I always make a copy of my pattern, enlarge it, and highlight (with a yellow marker) the numbers or instructions that relate to the size I am knitting. For example, when I see instructions that tell me to "increase 12 (12, 13, 14, 16, 17) stitches," I highlight the number that corresponds to the size of my sweater. That way, I know exactly what to do (or how many or how often), without being distracted by numbers that do not apply to me.

The sweater instructions may direct you to do something (for example, increase or decrease) every 8th row a certain number of times, again indicated by a series of numbers. If the directions for your size indicate that you should increase or decrease 0 number of times, you can just skip that step in the knitting instructions.

There are several easy ways to keep track of the specific instructions for your sweater. You may want to make a check list, keep a numerical tally, or count with a grocery clicker or row counter. Some patterns indicate how many stitches there should be at the beginning and end of a section of the garment (a sleeve, for example), which makes it easy to double-check that you have made the correct number of increases or decreases.

When knitting a neckline, the directions usually describe the shaping in terms of "every alternate row" or "every other row." As you shape a neckline, you need to knit two rows—one to knit to the shoulder and the other to return to the neck edge. Neckline directions may also read something like "every other row decrease 5 stitches once, 3 stitches twice, and then 1 stitch 4 times." You need to knit 2 rows for each decrease or group of decreases—so this shaping will require you to knit a total of 14 rows. The rate of decreasing can vary from size to size, so this is the kind of information you need to highlight for the size you are knitting.

When you need to repeat a set of instructions, the instructions usually begin with an asterisk (★) and are followed by a double asterisk (★★). A series of numbers indicates how often or how many times to repeat the instructions for each size of sweater.

Schematics

Schematics are the road map of a good knitting pattern. These drawings are labeled to indicate how many stitches or inches the various parts of the garment should be. The schematics also provide visual clues as to when and where to increase and decrease.

The schematic is helpful while knitting because it reinforces the written directions. It also supplies the measurements you'll need when blocking the finished garment to size (assuming your gauge is accurate) or when making alterations.

Initially, a schematic can also help you choose which size garment to knit. Pay close attention to the measurements of the garment pieces. Remember that all patterns allow for some ease—and

the bulkier the yarn, the more ease you need for a comfortable fit. Usually, a pattern assumes 4" to 6" (10 to 15 cm) of ease for most adult garments and 2" to 4" (5 to 10 cm) for children's. If you are unsure what size sweater to make, measure a sweater that has a fit that you like and compare its measurements to those in the schematic.

Each schematic also indicates the finished width, length, and measurement from center back to sleeve cuff so you can plan ahead for a perfect fit. When you are knitting cuff to cuff, you can usually add or subtract garment length (number of stitches within the body) without making any other major changes. The adjustment may change the number of stitches you'll need to pick up for cardigan bands and may affect stitch-patterning repeats, but you will not have to recalculate any of the garment shaping.

If you add to or subtract from the garment width (rows within the body), you can just absorb those changes into the shoulder areas without having to refigure the neck shaping. Changing garment width will affect the sleeve length, however. For example, adding rows to make the body wider will also make the sleeves longer. Knitting fewer rows will make the body narrower and the sleeves shorter.

To adjust sleeve length, you can usually add or subtract an inch or so before the first increase. Anything more drastic than that can be a problem because you will need to redistribute the increases (and decreases) to retain the shape of the sleeve. Of course, if you begin and end your sleeves with scrap knitting (pages 19–20), you can always add additional rows or lengthen or shorten the edge band to create the desired sleeve length.

Stitch Charts and Patterning

Unlike row-by-row written instructions, stitch charts give a quick visual impression of the stitches' relationship to each other and the pattern they will form. The charts in this book use the standard international symbols for knitting along with a text explanation.

Each row of the chart represents one row of fabric (unless otherwise stated), and each square represents one stitch *as seen from the right side of the fabric.* All of the right-side rows are read from right to left. All of the wrong-side rows are read from left to right.

Below is the chart for **stockinette stitch**. The chart indicates that all of the stitches on the right side of the fabric are knit stitches. So, to create this fabric, the stitches in the wrong-side rows must be worked as purl stitches if you are working on straight needles or working back and forth on a circular needle. If you are working in the round, all of the rounds, or rows, would be knitted.

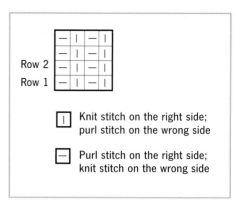

The third chart is for **garter stitch**. If you are knitting back and forth—on straight or circular needles—garter stitch is worked by knitting every row. As shown in the chart, the right side of the fabric will show alternating rounds of knit and purl. When you are working in the round on circular or double-pointed needles, you need to alternate knit rounds with purl to create a garter stitch fabric (circular work is never turned, and knitting every round would produce stockinette stitch).

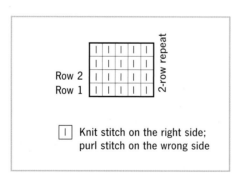

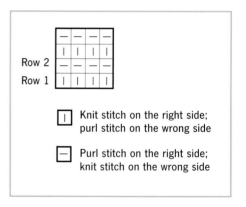

The next stitch chart is for **k1p1 ribbing**. The right-side and wrong-side rows are both worked by knitting one stitch and purling the next, so that purl stitches stack up over purl stitches and knit stitches over knit stitches on each side of the fabric.

The stitch chart for each of the fabrics shown above includes symbols for the unique stitches and techniques used to create that fabric. Don't rely on your memory to keep patterning consistent! It's a good idea to make a copy of the stitch chart for your garment so that you can check off rows as you work and make notes as needed. (You may want to use the original pattern again later for another size.)

When dividing the work to knit the front neckline, for example, you should make a note of the pattern row so that the pattern will be continuous when you begin work on the back neckline. When increasing for sleeves or for shaping necklines, incorporate the new stitches into the stitch patterning as soon as possible, but remember to always leave one plain edge stitch for seaming (pages 21–23).

Edge stitches should never be patterned. Simple knit and purl stitches will help maintain an even, smooth edge that makes it easy to join perfect seams. For most of the sweaters in this book, you will begin every row by slipping the first stitch as if to purl (that is, with the yarn in front of the needle). You will always knit the last stitch in the row through the back loop, regardless of the stitch pattern. When you need to handle the edge stitches differently (for example, when changing color in the children's Classic Stripes sweater, page 50), there will be specific instructions in the pattern notes.

Weekend Woodsman (page 32) is a simple six-stitch repeat of knits and purls.

Autumn Leaves (page 56) is an allover pattern created with a specific texture stitch.

The decorative stitches in Fan Dancer (page 68) form alternating "fans" of grouped stitches.

CHAPTER THREE

Starting and Finishing

Through my experience as a machine knitter, I have picked up quite a few good tricks for hand knitting. One trick I strongly recommend is scrap knitting at the beginning and end of the knitting. With scrap knitting, you can retain "live," or open, stitches that you can pick up later to create bands or edgings.

If you plan from the start, you can also join the live stitches in smooth, bulk-free seams. Live stitches can always be bound off if you eventually change your mind about the finishing details.

Provisional cast-ons usually provide only a crocheted chain base or a twisted cord to secure the first row of stitches. I find these cast-ons difficult to manage because the stitches tend to be irregular and difficult to find when I go back to pick them up later. With a conventional cast-on, you can't turn the edge into a row of live stitches, so I opt for the flexibility provided by scrap knitting.

To start a fabric with scrap yarn, cast on with the simple looped cast-on (page 90). Always choose a yarn that is close to the same size as your main yarn, contrasts well with it, and won't leave any telltale fuzz when removed. Knit two or three rows of scrap yarn before switching to the main yarn. It is much easier to find and pick up the

stitches if you have several rows of scrap knitting below them. The first row that you knit with the main yarn is then an actual row, not a cast-on edge.

At the other end of the piece, work two or three rows of scrap knitting and bind off. It may seem like a waste of time to bind off yarn that will ultimately be removed, but the bind-off keeps the stitches snug and secure until you get back to them—even if the sweater sits in a basket for years waiting to be finished!

Scrap knitting provides an inexpensive, flexible, readily available stitch holder that can accommodate any number of stitches. The knitting is not removed until the garment edge has been seamed, ribbed, crocheted, bound, or otherwise finished and checked. Press the scrap yarn

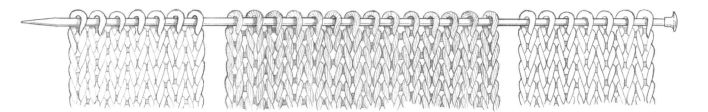

If the color of the scrap-knitting yarn (white) strongly contrasts with the color of the main yarn (shaded), the stitches stand out clearly and are easy to pick up when the scrap is folded back.

to help it lie flat and then simply fold it back and work through the exposed main stitches. Grafting invisible seams from a piece of scrap knitting is a piece of cake, and the "gourmet" hand-sewn bind-off (see page 35) is much easier when worked off scrap knitting than it is when worked directly off the needles.

When I knit cuff-to-cuff sweaters, I seldom cast on or bind off sleeves, center front, or side body edges with the main yarn. Using scrap ensures that the two sleeve edges match (instead of one being cast on and the other bound off) and gives me live stitches for the front bands and for invisible side seams. Having live stitches also enables me to add length or change details after the sweater is knitted. Although I prefer scrapping on and off, that doesn't mean that it is the only right way to knit these sweaters. If you are more comfortable casting on and binding off with the main yarn, by all means, do it that way. Just read through the pattern first to make sure there aren't any finishing details that will require live stitches.

Scrapping On

When you have completed the right sleeve of your cuff-to-cuff garment, you need to add stitches to either side of it to knit the body of the sweater. Cut the main yarn. Push the sleeve to the center

of the circular needle and leave it there.

With scrap yarn, cast on the required number of stitches at one end of the needle and knit several rows of stock-inette stitch. Work the scrap knitting so that the right side of the scrap is on the same side of the knitting as the right side of the sleeve—this way, it will be easier to see the stitches when you fold back the scrap to pick them up. Cut the scrap yarn. Then cast on and knit another section of scrap knitting at the other end of the needle, as shown in the drawing. When you have knit the same number of scrap rows on this end, cut the scrap yarn. Work the main yarn at one end of the needle across *all* of the stitches (scrap, sleeve, and scrap).

If you're working on straight needles, cast on the required number of stitches with scrap at the beginning of the row. Then work a couple of rows back and forth on the scrap stitches only. Cut the scrap yarn. Reattach the main yarn and knit 1 row across the scrap and the sleeve stitches. Do not cut the main yarn. Cast on with the scrap at the end of the row and work a couple of rows over the scrap stitches only, ending with the scrap stitches on the left needle and the rest of the stitches on the right needle. Cut the scrap and then finish the first row with the main yarn by working across the scrap stitches.

Scrapping Off

When you finish knitting the body of the sweater, you need to remove stitches at either end of the needle to continue knitting the sleeve on the center stitches. Cut the main yarn. With scrap yarn, knit across the specified number of stitches that need to be removed at one end of the needle. Turn (do not wrap), and work back to the beginning of the row. Work two more rows and then bind off the scrap knitting. Repeat the same process at the other end of the needle.

If you're using straight needles, work the main yarn across the first group of stitches that need to be removed. Drop the main yarn and work a couple of rows of scrap knitting back and forth across the same stitches. Bind off the scrap knitting. With the main yarn, work only across the stitches that will be start the sleeve. Work the remainder of the row with scrap yarn. Work back and forth with scrap yarn for a couple of rows and then bind off the scrap knitting. Begin working the sleeve with the main yarn.

Finishing Considerations

I've always believed that finishing notes should come at the beginning of sweater patterns. The way the sweater is knitted actually determines the ways in which it can be finished. If you choose one knitting method over another, you may find that when it comes time to finish your sweater, you have unintentionally limited your options. So, check all the pattern notes in the instructions for the individual sweaters before you even pick up your needles!

Before you begin finishing and assembling your sweater, secure any yarn tails that you will not use for stitching seams. Work the tails back into the knitting, as shown in the drawing below. I usually leave fairly long tails, which can then be used to seam the pieces, thus avoiding the need to start a new yarn just for seaming. To keep these long tails from tangling while I knit, I wind figure eights around my thumb and forefinger, and then tie the yarn end around the center of the eight to hold the strands together.

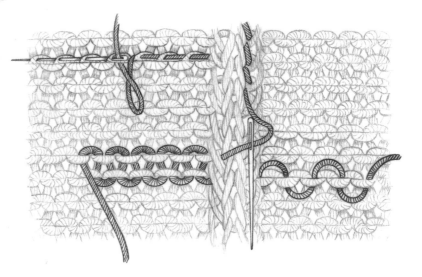

Working tails back into the knitting

Blocking

Blocking is an important part of the sweater-making process as it determines the final size and shape of the garment and also enhances the finished look. Although you can sometimes coax the fabric a bit to make up for pieces that are a tad too narrow or wide, don't expect to correct major problems in the knitting by blocking.

Blocking can be as simple a process as covering the sweater pieces with damp towels or holding a steam iron over them and patting them into shape. I block everything I knit to exact size on a large padded surface that has a gridded cover marked with 1" (2.5 cm) squares. You can also block knitting on top of an ironing board or on several layers of towels or old blankets.

Ideally, you should work on a surface into which you can insert pins. I use pins with large, easy-to-see heads to pin the garment pieces, face down, to the exact measurements shown in the sweater schematic. Then I hold my steam iron about 1" (2.5 cm) above the fabric and saturate the entire piece with steam, without ever resting the iron directly on the knitting. (There are some yarns, however, that specifically require that you "press hard." Scrap knitting also behaves best when pressed flat.)

You'll need a lot of pins when blocking. Space them no more than 1" (2.5 cm) apart all around the piece. You can also work with just a few pins and blocking wires—thin wires that are inserted into the edges of the knitting. Blocking wires are easier to use when manipulating large pieces and they produce much smoother edges. It takes more time to thread the wires through the edges of the fabric, but the end result is worth it.

When the blocked pieces cool and dry, remove the pins. You'll find that the knitting is much easier to handle. The edges lie flat, the yarn has "bloomed" to fill out the stitches, and the stitches are well aligned. Blocking also guarantees that the side edges or sleeves edges of both the front and the back are the same length, which is essential when seaming.

About Seams

The fabrics for many of the sweaters in this book look just as good on the purl side as on the knit side, so it is really up to you which you choose as the right side of the sweater.

You don't actually have to decide which is which while you are knitting, but you do need to decide before you start seaming the sweater and working in the tails.

All garments require some seaming, even if it's only a couple of basic stitches to join selvages, bound-off edges, or open stitches. Always work with a blunt metal or plastic needle to avoid splitting the yarn as you seam.

Almost without exception, I work all my increases and decreases one stitch from the edge, and I never work them as part of any stitch patterning. In this way, I create a consistent seam stitch, which makes it easy and quick to construct perfectly straight seams. If you don't allow for these plain edge stitches, the garment's seams jog in and out with every decrease or change in stitch patterning. Adding this one trick to your repertoire can make all the difference in your finishing!

To seam selvage edges, I prefer the invisible seam created by the mattress stitch. This stitch is always worked on the right side of the garment, regardless

Seaming knit stitches

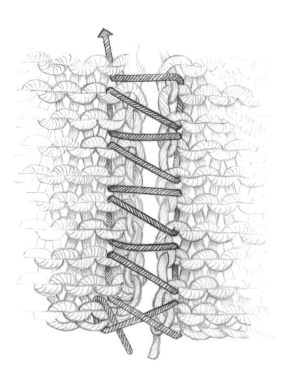

Seaming purl stitches

of whether the surface of the right side is made up of knit or purl stitches. If you leave a long enough tail when you begin, you can actually use the tail to sew your seam—which reduces the number of ends you need to hide later. I always work a figure-eight stitch at the base of the seam to align the edges and add enough texture to mimic the cast-on edge. Although a mattress-stitch seam is not the flattest seam there is, it always looks perfect on the outside of the garment.

When seaming knit stitches, pass the needle under two of the horizontal bars between the first and second column of stitches, then exit the fabric. Now pass the needle under two bars on the other side. Always return the needle to the last place it exited on the opposite side, always one full stitch from the edge (see top drawing at left). Continue working side to side, loosely seaming about six to eight stitches. Then tug the yarn gently to bring the two edges of the seam together. This technique works better

than tightening each stitch as you go—
it's easier to see where you have stitched
and where you need to stitch next.

When seaming purl stitches, insert the
needle into the lower loop of the purl
stitch on one side of the seam and into
the upper loop of the corresponding
stitch on the other side (see bottom
drawing on the facing page).

You can also secure bound-off or
selvage edges with backstitching or slip
crochet, as shown at right.

Grafting, also called Kitchener stitch,
is used to join live stitches in invisible
seams. The effect mimics a row of knitting and requires even tension for a
perfect finish. You can graft stitches
directly from two knitting needles, with
the knitting lying flat on a table, but I
prefer working from scrap knitting. Press
the scrap knitting (not the sweater) and
fold it back so that you can see the live
stitches. Then thread a yarn needle with
a length of the main yarn—at least twice
the width of the piece you are grafting—and begin sewing in and out of the
stitches as shown in the drawing below.

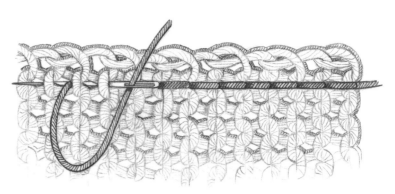

Backstitching

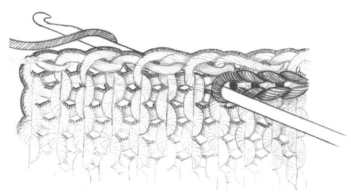

Slip crochet

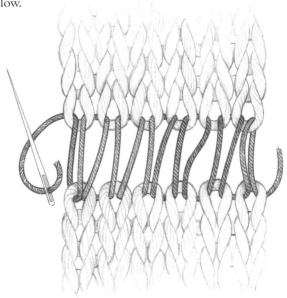

Grafting or Kitchener stitch

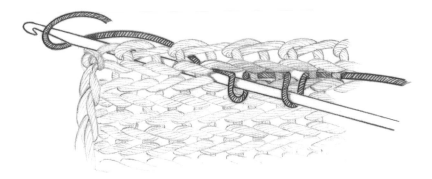

Picking up stitches along selvage edge

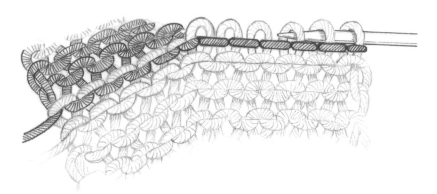

Picking up stitches from scrap

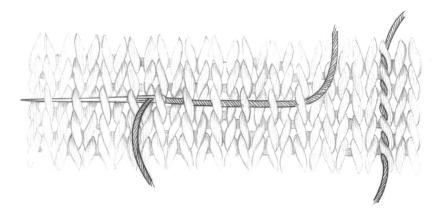

Marking the fabric to pick up stitches from the surface

Picking Up Stitches

Most patterns will tell you *approximately* how many stitches to pick up from selvage edges to create bands. The rule of thumb is to pick up about two-thirds as many stitches as there are rows—although some sources recommend three-fourths as many stitches as rows. Unless you are working a specific pattern stitch, a few stitches more or less won't matter.

The most important things are that the sweater fit over the wearer's head and that the lower edge is not gathered too tightly (because of too few stitches) or flaring (because of too many). If you are picking up live stitches from scrap knitting, make sure that you account for every stitch. Be careful not to twist the stitches as you feed them onto the needle. Double-check your work before removing the scrap knitting.

You can pick up stitches either with a knitting needle or a crochet hook. I also have a 32" (approximately 82 cm) circular Turbo Cro-Needle (made by Addi), which combines the two (see Sources of Supply, page 93). It has a #2 crochet hook on one end and a #3 knitting needle on the other. You pick up stitches with the hook end and knit them off the other end onto a regular needle. When you need to pick up a lot of stitches, this tool simplifies and speeds up the process.

With the right side facing you, insert the needle or the hook through the edge of the fabric—consistently one full or one half-stitch from the edge—and bring up a loop (see top drawing on the facing

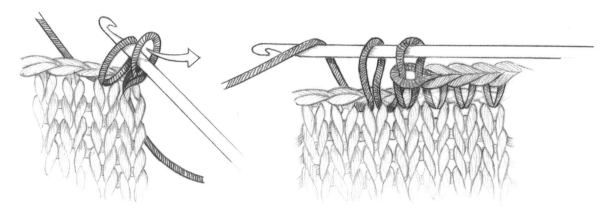

Slip Crochet

Single crochet edging

page). Push the loop back on the needle and, working to the left, insert the needle into the next space in the fabric edge. When you have picked up all of the stitches, work one plain row and then begin the rib or other band.

Picking up stitches from scrap knitting is easiest if the scrap knitting has been pressed first. The scrap will fold back smoothly, and the first row of live stitches will pop right up. Simply insert the needle through the stitches, as shown in the center drawing on the facing page, so they are not twisted on the needle.

You can knit pockets, flaps, and decorative appliqués directly onto the surface of a garment by picking up stitches across a row or column of stitches, as shown in the bottom drawing on the facing page.

Crochet Finishing

You can also finish edges with decorative crochet. All you need is a couple of basic stitches. Single crochet is a good choice for the first row of most edgings—or on its own for a simpler finish. Insert the hook consistently through either a whole or a half-edge stitch to bring up a loop of yarn. Pull the loop back through to the front of the work and form another loop with the hook. Pull that loop through the two loops already on the hook (see drawing, above right).

There are lots of ways to approach finishing—and several options for every technique—but with experience, we all find the methods that work best for us. Remember to always practice any new techniques on your gauge swatch before trying them on the sweater itself.

The Twelve Sweaters

crayon stripes

Knitting the basic cuff-to-cuff sweater with a space-dyed yarn automatically creates vertical, shaded stripes. The narrow ribbed bands are finished with a gently rolled edge. This is the basic side-to-side silhouette.

Featured Design Variations

- Crew neck
- Bands in k1p1 rib with a lightly rolled edge
- Stockinette stitch work (so the knit side is the right side)

Yarn: Noro "Kureyon" (100% wool with 92 yards/84 meters or 1.75 ounce/50 gram skein), color #90, 8 (8, 9, 9, 10, 10) skeins

Needles: Size US 5/3.75 mm and US 7/4.5 mm needles OR SIZE TO OBTAIN GAUGE

Notions: tapestry needle, tape measure, 2 stitch holders

Gauge: 20 stitches and 28 rows = 4" (10 cm) in stockinette stitch

Sizes: Women's XS (S, M, L, XL, XXL). *Model is wearing size M.*

Finished Measurements:

Garment width: 17 (18, 20, 22, 24, 26)"/43 (46, 51, 56, 61, 66) cm

Garment length: 20 (20.5, 21, 21.5, 22, 22)"/51 (52, 53, 55, 56, 56) cm

Center back to sleeve cuff: 26.5 (27, 28, 29, 30, 31)"/67 (69, 71, 74, 76, 79) cm

Stitch Chart

Row 1
Row 2

2-row repeat

☐ Knit stitch on the right side; purl stitch on the wrong side

Step 1

With the smaller needles, cast on 46 (46, 46, 46, 50, 50) stitches and work 5 rows stockinette stitch, then 7 rows of k1p1 rib. The purl side of the stockinette rolled edge is the right side (the knit side of the fabric is the right side of the garment itself). Change to the larger needles and continue in stockinette stitch, increasing 0 (0, 0, 2, 0, 2) stitches evenly across the first row. Work until the sleeve measures 18" (46 cm) from the beginning, *at the same time* increasing 1 stitch each end of every 8th row 7 (0, 2, 0, 0, 0) times, every 6th row 10 (18, 10, 10, 8, 8) times, and every 4th row 0 (2, 10, 14, 17, 17) times. 80 (86, 90, 96, 100, 102) stitches.

Step 2

Using either the cable cast-on or the simple looped cast-on method, cast on 60 stitches, then knit across these stitches and the sleeve stitches to cast on 60 stitches at the other end of the row (or see page 19 for scrap method). There should be 200 (206, 210, 216, 220, 222) stitches on the needle. Work 5 (5.5, 6.5, 7.25, 8.25, 9)"/13 (14, 16.5, 18.5, 21, 23) cm to complete the first shoulder. Then work one row across 100 (103, 105, 108, 110, 111) stitches, ending at the neckline/shoulder. Place the remaining 100 (103, 105, 108, 110, 111) stitches on a holder for knitting the back of the sweater.

18" (46 cm)

3.25 (3.25, 3.5, 3.5, 3.5, 3.5)"/
8.5 (8.5, 9, 9, 9, 9) cm

16 (16, 18, 18, 18, 18)"/
41, (41, 46, 46, 46, 46) cm

7 (7, 7, 7, 7.5, 7.5,
8)"/18 (18, 19,
19, 20.5) cm

5 (5.5, 6.5, 7.25, 8.25,
9)"/13 (14, 16.5, 18.5,
21, 23) cm

17 (18, 20, 22, 24, 26)"/43 (46, 51, 56, 61, 66) cm

16 (17, 18, 19, 20, 20.5)"/41 (43, 46, 48, 51, 52) cm
80 (86, 90, 96, 100, 100) sts

12"/30.5 cm
60 sts

9 (9, 9, 9.5, 10, 10.5)"/23 (23, 23, 24, 25.5, 27) cm
46 (46, 46, 46, 50, 50) sts

Step 3

Working only on the front 100 (103, 105, 108, 110, 111) stitches, shape the front neckline as follows: At the beginning of the next row, bind off 4 stitches. Then at the beginning of the following alternate rows, bind off at the neck edge 3 stitches once, 2 stitches twice, and 1 stitch 5 (5, 7, 7, 7, 7) times. 84 (87, 87, 90, 92, 93) stitches remain. Work 2" (5 cm) straight. Every other row at the neck edge, cast on 1 stitch 5 (5, 7, 7, 7, 7) times, 2 stitches twice, 3 stitches once, and 4 stitches once. 100 (103, 105, 108, 110, 111) stitches. Place the front stitches on a holder.

Step 4

Return the back stitches to the needle and continue knitting on the back stitches alone for 7 (7, 7, 7.5, 7.5, 8)"/ 18 (18, 18, 19, 19, 20.5) cm. Return the front stitches to the needle and knit across all stitches for 5 (5.5, 6.5, 7.25, 8.25, 9)"/13 (14, 16.5, 18.5, 21, 23) cm to complete the second shoulder.

Step 5

At the beginning of the next two rows, bind off 60 stitches (or see page 20 for scrap method). 80 (86, 90, 96, 100, 102) stitches remain. Knit the sleeve for 16.5" (42 cm), decreasing 1 stitch each end of every 4th row 0 (2, 10, 14, 17, 17) times, every 6th row 10 (18, 10, 10, 8, 8) times, and every 8th row 7 (0, 2, 0, 0, 0) times. Decrease 0 (0, 0, 2, 0, 2) stitches evenly across the last row. Change to the smaller needles and work 7 rows k1p1 rib, followed by 5 rows stockinette. Bind off loosely.

Finishing

Block the garment piece. With the smaller needle and the right side of the garment facing you, and beginning at left shoulder, pick up and knit 16 (16, 16, 18, 18, 18) stitches along the first side of the front neck, 8 stitches at the center, 16 (16, 16, 18, 18, 18) stitches along the second side, and then 32 (32, 32, 35, 35, 37) stitches from the back.

Work 7 rows k1p1 rib and then 5 rows stockinette. Bind off loosely.

Sew the sleeve seams and the side seams. With the smaller needle and the right side facing you, and beginning at one side seam, pick up and knit 158 (166, 186, 204, 222, 240) stitches around lower edge of the sweater. Work 7 rows k1p1 and then 5 rows stockinette. Bind off loosely. Work in all yarn tails.

Rolled Rib Bands

The edges of stockinette and stockinette-based fabrics tend to roll unless they are finished with bands that stabilize them. Various ribs, garter stitch, and I-cord edgings are commonly used, with specific ones chosen because they complement the stitch work or yarn used for the body of a garment. You can, however, simply allow the edge of a garment to roll. Plain rolled edges do tend to stretch after a while, so I almost always use some rib between the roll and the garment—even just two rows of rib will do the trick. A single ridge of garter stitch will help define the edge and can be a good place to hide increases if you work the roll on fewer stitches. You may choose to knit enough rows for a full, closed roll or just a few rows that create a reverse stockinette edge before a rib. You can introduce a different color or texture for the rolled edge or work buttonholes in the rolled front edge of a cardigan.

Always work the rolled edge treatment as part of your swatch so you can accurately determine just how many rows it will take for the fabric to roll and how those rows will or won't affect the length of the garment itself. Remember that the fabric always rolls with the purl side showing, which is important to know if you are combining the rolled edge with stitch patterning that has a definite right and wrong side.

Make sure that the cast-on is not so firm that it pulls in and prevents the edge from rolling easily. I like to use a simple looped cast-on because it is loose and stretchy and disappears inside the roll. When binding off a rolled edge, I usually use a simple back stitch. Rolled edges should be worked on smaller needles than those you use for the body of a garment so that the edge is firm, well defined, and holds its shape. It also helps to work on about 10 percent fewer stitches than the first row of the sleeve calls for, which is often the formula for ribs. You could easily substitute a roll for a rib—just make sure you take the final sleeve length into consideration.

weekend woodsman

A simple pattern of knit and purl stitches interrupts the color runs in the yarn and creates a rich visual texture in this comfortable classic.

Featured Design Variations

- Shaped front and back necklines
- k2p2 rib bands
- Knit/purl stitch *work*

Yarn: Mountain Colors "4/8's Wool" (100% wool with 250 yards/229 meters per 3.5 ounce/100 gram skein), Pheasant, 6 (6, 7, 7, 8) skeins

Needles: Size US 5/3.75 mm and US 7/4.5 mm needles OR SIZE TO OBTAIN GAUGE

US 5/3.75 mm circular needle 16"/40 cm long for neck edge

Gauge: 20 stitches and 28 rows = 4" (10 cm) in pattern stitch

Notions: stitch holders, tape measure, tapestry needle

Size: Men's S (M, L, XL, XXL). *Model is wearing size L.*

Finished Measurements:

Garment width: 20 (22, 24, 26, 28)"/51 (56, 61, 66, 71) cm

Garment length: 25 (26.5, 28, 29.5, 31)"/63.5 (67.5, 71, 75, 79) cm

Center back neck to sleeve cuff: 28 (30, 31.5, 33, 34.5)"/71 (76, 80, 84, 88) cm

Notes: (1) Row 1 of the chart is a wrong-side, purl, row. (2) Maintain 1 plain edge stitch throughout. See page 17 for detail of stitch pattern.

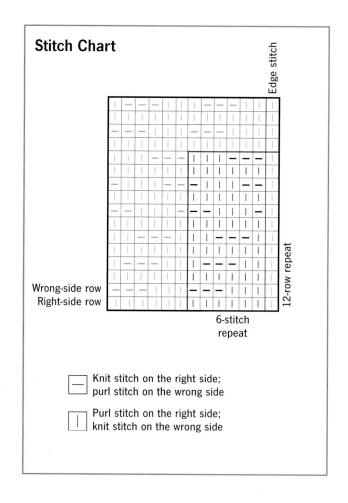

Stitch Chart

Edge stitch

Wrong-side row
Right-side row

6-stitch repeat

12-row repeat

☐ Knit stitch on the right side; purl stitch on the wrong side

| Purl stitch on the right side; knit stitch on the wrong side

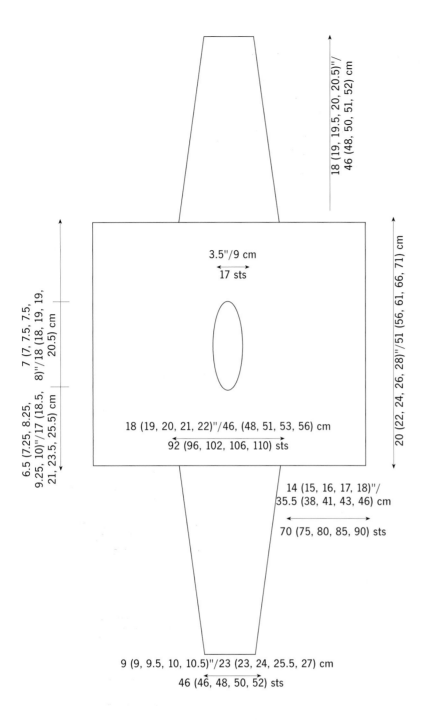

18 (19, 19.5, 20, 20.5)"/
46 (48, 50, 51, 52) cm

3.5"/9 cm
17 sts

20 (22, 24, 26, 28)"/51 (56, 61, 66, 71) cm

18 (19, 20, 21, 22)"/46, (48, 51, 53, 56) cm
92 (96, 102, 106, 110) sts

7 (7, 7.5, 7.5,
8)"/18 (18, 19, 19,
20.5) cm

6.5 (7.25, 8.25,
9.25, 10)"/17 (18.5,
21, 23.5, 25.5) cm

14 (15, 16, 17, 18)"/
35.5 (38, 41, 43, 46) cm

70 (75, 80, 85, 90) sts

9 (9, 9.5, 10, 10.5)"/23 (23, 24, 25.5, 27) cm
46 (46, 48, 50, 52) sts

Step 1

With the MC and the smaller needle, cast on 42 (42, 42, 46, 46) stitches and work k2p2 rib for 2" (5 cm), increasing 4 (4, 6, 4, 6) stitches evenly across the last row. 46 (46, 48, 50, 52) stitches. Change to the larger needle and work in pattern until the sleeve measures 18 (19, 19.5, 20, 20.5)"/46 (48, 50, 51, 52) cm from the start, *at the same time*

increasing 1 stitch each end of every 6th row 17 (15, 13, 13, 13) times, then every 4th row 6 (10, 14, 15, 16) times. When incorporating increased stitches into the pattern, continue to maintain 1 plain edge stitch. End with a wrong side row. 92 (96, 102, 106, 110) stitches.

Step 2

At the end of the next two rows, cast on 70 (75, 80, 85, 90) stitches and, maintaining pattern, work 6.5 (7.25, 8.25, 9.25, 10)"/16.5 (18.5, 21, 23.5, 25.5) cm for first shoulder. Slip all of the back stitches to a holder to continue on the front stitches only. Make a note on the chart of the pattern row when the work divides.

Step 3

Shape the front neckline by binding off at the neck edge, every other row, 5 stitches once, 4 stitches once, 3 stitches once, 2 stitches twice, and 1 stitch once. 17 stitches decreased. Work 24 (24, 28, 28, 32) rows straight. Begin increasing at the neck edge by casting on, every other row, 1 stitch once, 2 stitches twice, 3 stitches once, 4 stitches once, and 5 stitches once. 17 stitches increased. Make note of the pattern row and slip all of the front stitches to a holder.

Step 4

Return the back stitches to the needle and, continuing pattern, shape the back neckline by binding off at the neck edge, every other row, 2 stitches twice then 1 stitch once. Work 36 (36, 40, 40, 44) rows straight. Begin increasing the neckline by casting on, every other row, 1 stitch once then 2 stitches twice. Return the front stitches to the needle. Both pieces should be on the same pattern row. If not, add or subtract a row from the front or back so that the pattern is continuous, then work across all stitches to complete the second shoulder the same as the first.

Step 5

At the beginning of the next 2 rows, bind off 70 (75, 80, 85, 90) stitches and shape the second sleeve by decreasing 1 stitch each end of every 4th row 6 (10, 14, 15, 16) times then every 6th row 17 (15, 13, 13, 13) times. Continue to maintain 1 plain edge stitch. When the sleeve measures 16 (17, 17.5, 18, 18.5)"/41 (43, 44.5, 46, 47) cm, decrease 4 (4, 6, 4, 6) stitches evenly across the last row. Change to the smaller needle and work k2p2 rib for 2" (5 cm). Bind off loosely.

Finishing

Block the garment piece. With the smaller needle, pick up approximately 45 (45, 47, 47, 49) stitches from the front neckline and 35 (35, 37, 37, 39) from the back neckline to work 1.5" (4 cm) k2p2 rib. Bind off loosely.

Sew the sleeve and side seams. With the smaller needle and the MC, pick up approximately 186 (204, 221, 244, 260) stitches around the lower edge and work k2p2 rib for 2" (5 cm). Bind off loosely and work in all yarn tails.

Gourmet Bind-Off

The hand-sewn, "gourmet" bind-off produces a very refined edge that really retains its elasticity. Although it takes a little more time to knit than a conventional rib bind-off, the final result is worth it—and the little channel formed at the edge is perfect for inserting elastic thread in cotton ribs! This bind-off can be worked on either k1p1 or k2p2 ribs.

Hand-knitting instructions for this bind-off say to work directly off the knitting needle. I was never able to master the technique until I began machine knitting. Machine knitters end their ribs with scrap knitting and then work the bind-off by hand through the scrap. It was a "Eureka!" moment for me and has become the only way I use or teach this method.

After working the band with the main yarn, cut the yarn and leave a tail about three times the width of the ribbing. Then work three rows of scrap knitting. The first row is worked *knit 1, slip 1** for k1p1 rib or *knit 2, slip 2** for k2p2 rib, repeating from * to ** across the row.

Purl all the stitches in the second row and knit the third row. The scrap can be bound off or the needle can remain in the last row of stitches. Press the scrap knitting so it lies flat and then fold it back. Because of the slipped stitches in the first row of scrap, the rib stitches present themselves in two distinct rows.

Thread a tapestry needle with the tail of the main yarn. Work back and forth from one row to the next, always working each stitch twice by inserting the needle into the same stitch that it last exited in that row. When working the "top" row of stitches, sew a U by entering down through one stitch and up the next. When working the "bottom" row of stitches, the stitch is an upside-down U as the needle is inserted up through the first stitch and down through the second. Avoid overtightening each stitch—you simply want to mimic the tension of the other stitches. Clip the scrap and gently pull it through the edge to remove it.

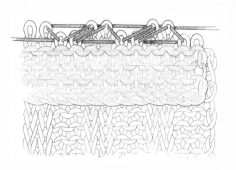

Work each stitch twice, always reinserting the needle into the same stitch you last exited on the opposite side. The method mimics grafting.

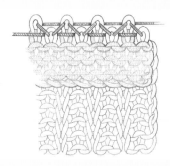

The stitches seem to slant while you are working this bind-off, but they align perfectly after the scrap is removed. Be careful not to work too tightly or the edge will pucker.

chiquita jacketta

With simple shaping, thick yarn, and big needles, this jacket is quick and easy to knit in stockinette, with the knit side as the right side of the garment. The V-shaped section at front center, knitted in seed stitch, forms a self-collar.

Featured Design Variations

- Self-collar that tapers into front bands
- Turn-back cuffs
- Patch pockets picked up and knit on sweater fronts
- Loose, large-button closure

Yarn: Colinette "Point 5" (100% wool with approximately 54 yards/50 meters per 3.5 ounce/100 gram skein), MC #124, Celadon, 8 (9, 9, 10, 10, 11) skeins, Colinette "Wigwam" (100% cotton with 142 yards/130 meters per 3.5 ounce/100 gram skein), CC1 #113, Velvet Leaf, 2 skeins, and 1 skein smooth cotton or acrylic in contrasting color for scrap yarn

Gauge: 9 stitches and 11 rows = 4" (10 cm) in stockinette

Needles: Size US 17/12.75 mm and US 10/6 mm OR SIZE TO OBTAIN GAUGE; double-pointed size US 10/6mm optional for sleeves

Notions: tape measure, tapestry needle, 1 large button (I used JHB's #80014 lizard.)

Sizes: Women's XS (S, M, L, XL, XXL). *Model is wearing size L.*

Notes:

I find that when I work on jumbo needles (such as US 17/12.5 mm), I often obtain very different gauges on circular and straight needles. It is best not to switch back and forth within the same garment unless you check your gauge on both. Also, straight needles will probably not be long enough to accommodate all of the stitches for the three largest sizes.

Work all sleeve increases and decreases one stitch from the edge for neater seams.

Finished Measurements:

Garment width: 18 (19, 20, 22, 24, 26)"/46 (48, 51, 56, 61, 66) cm

Garment length: 20.5 (21, 21.5, 22, 22, 22.5)"/52 (53, 55, 56, 56, 57) cm

Center back to sleeve cuff: 26 (26.5, 27, 28, 29, 30)"/66 (67, 69, 71, 74, 76) cm

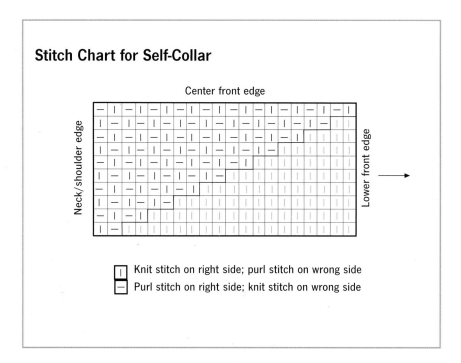

Stitch Chart for Self-Collar

- ⊟ Knit stitch on right side; purl stitch on wrong side
- ⊡ Purl stitch on right side; knit stitch on wrong side

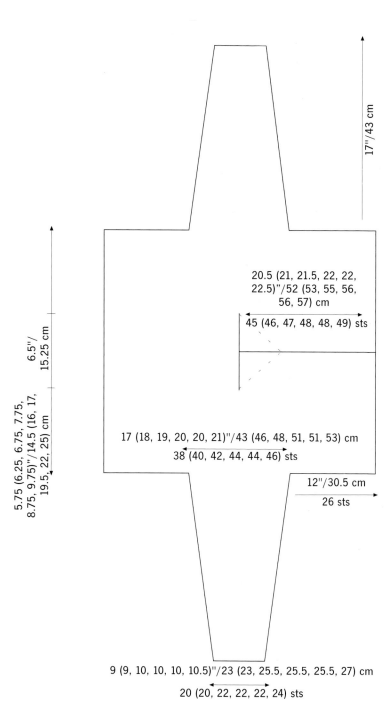

17"/43 cm

20.5 (21, 21.5, 22, 22, 22.5)"/52 (53, 55, 56, 56, 57) cm

45 (46, 47, 48, 48, 49) sts

18 (19, 20, 22, 24, 26)"/ 46 (48, 51, 56, 61, 66) cm

6.5"/ 15.25 cm

5.75 (6.25, 6.75, 7.75, 8.75, 9.75)"/14.5 (16, 17, 19.5, 22, 25) cm

17 (18, 19, 20, 20, 21)"/43 (46, 48, 51, 51, 53) cm

38 (40, 42, 44, 44, 46) sts

12"/30.5 cm

26 sts

9 (9, 10, 10, 10, 10.5)"/23 (23, 25.5, 25.5, 25.5, 27) cm

20 (20, 22, 22, 22, 24) sts

Step 1

With the larger needles and the scrap yarn, cast on 20 (20, 22, 22, 22, 24) stitches and knit 2 rows. Change to the main yarn and, working in stockinette, knit the right sleeve for 17" (43 cm), at the same time increasing 1 stitch each end of every 6th row 4 (8, 8, 0, 0, 0) times and every 4th row 5 (2, 2, 11, 11, 11) times, working increases 1 stitch from the edge. Cut the main yarn.

Step 2

With the scrap yarn (page 19), cast on 26 stitches at one end of the needle and knit two rows. Cut the yarn and repeat at the other end of the needle. With the main yarn, work across all 90 (92, 94, 96, 96, 98) stitches until the shoulder measures 5.75 (6.25, 6.75, 7.75, 8.75, 9.75)"/14.5 (16, 17, 19.5, 22, 25) cm.

Step 3

Use two balls of yarn to knit the front and back necks at the same time. Work across the first 45 (46, 47, 48, 48, 49) front stitches with one ball and then across the remaining 45 (46, 47, 48, 48, 49) back stitches with the second ball. The back stitches are worked in stockinette, but the front stitches are progressively worked in seed stitch as shown in the stitch chart. When the front neckline measures 3.25" (8.5 cm), scrap off the right front stitches. With scrap, immediately cast on 45 (46, 47, 48, 48, 49) stitches for the left front. Knit two rows, change to the main yarn, and work the seed stitch pattern in reverse for the left front and stockinette for the back until the left front matches the right front.

Step 4

With one ball of the main yarn, work continuously across all front and back stitches again to knit the left shoulder to match the right shoulder. Scrap off (page 20) 26 stitches at each end of the needle.

Step 5

On the remaining 38 (40, 42, 44, 44, 46) stitches, work the left sleeve to 17" (43 cm), *at the same time* decreasing 1 stitch each end of every 4th row 5 (2, 2, 11, 11, 11) times and every 6th row 4 (8, 8, 0, 0, 0) times. Scrap off the remaining 20 (20, 22, 22, 22, 24) stitches.

Finishing

Lightly block the garment piece, but press the scrap knitting flat.

If you are *not* using double-pointed needles, fold back the scrap knitting at the end of one sleeve and slip the stitches onto the smaller needle. Because of the difference in size between the MC and the CC, you need to increase the number of stitches by knitting into every other stitch twice in the first row. That is, knit into the front and then the back of every other stitch. 30 (30, 33, 33, 33, 36) stitches. To work the corrugated band, *purl the next 2 rows and knit the following 2 rows.** Repeat from * to ** 7 more times and then bind off loosely.

If you are using double-pointed needles (which eliminates a cuff seam), the sleeve band is worked after the sleeve seam is joined. After the seam is joined, pick up the cuff stitches from scrap, distributing them evenly on four needles. Increase in every other stitch so there are 30 (30, 33, 33, 33, 36) stitches. Alternately purl 2 rounds then knit 2 rounds 8 times. Bind off loosely.

Sew the sleeve seams and graft the side seams. With the right side of the garment facing you, the smaller needles and CC1, pick up approximately 100 (104, 110, 120, 132, 144) stitches along the lower edge, working from one front edge to the other and picking up 1 stitch for every row. Knit the first row and then work the corrugated band for 2 1/2 repeats and bind off loosely.

Before beginning the front bands/collar, place markers at the base of the seed stitch on each front and at the corners of the collar (upper front edge/neck). Fold back the scrap knitting at the front edges and slip those stitches onto an extra needle. With the smaller needle and the MC, pick up and knit approximately 6 stitches from the end of the lower band, 67 (69, 70, 72, 72, 73) stitches along one front edge, 56 around the neck, 67 (69, 70, 72, 72, 73) stitches along the second front edge, and 6 stitches from the lower band, working every alternate stitch (on the front edges only) twice to compensate for the difference in yarn size.

When picking up below the seed stitch markers, pick up and knit. When working above the markers (in other words, the entire collar and neckline), pick up and *purl* those stitches to reverse the right and wrong sides of the fabric when the collar rolls to the outside. The band is worked from lower edge to lower edge, shaping the collar by increasing 1 stitch *every row* at the markers for the corners of the collar. Purl the first row, beginning with a wrong side row. Work 4 rows of the corrugated band and then make a 4-stitch buttonhole in the right band, even with the marker at the base of the seed stitch.

Work 2 more rows after the buttonhole and then begin shaping the collar with short rows as follows: Work the next row from the lower edge of one front to the seed stitch marker on the other front. Wrap, turn, and work back to the seed stitch marker on the other side. ★Wrap, turn, and work 10 stitches less then the previous row.★★ Repeat from ★ to ★★ until there are 6 working stitches at center back. Turn and work across all stitches to the lower edge, taking care to knit the wraps with the stitches.

Loosely bind off the entire front/ neckline, taking care to work the wraps with the stitches as you bind off the second side of the neckline as shown for Short-Row Knitting, page 85.

Sew a button directly to the left front or make a short I-cord on 2 needles (see page 71). Work 1.5" (4 cm) of I-cord, slip the stitches off the needle, enlarge them slightly, and thread them through the two holes in the button.

Cut the working yarn, leaving about 24" (61 cm) to work with, and then thread it through to the back of the button. Slip the stitches back onto the needle and continue working the I-cord for another inch (2.5 cm). Bind off by pulling the tail through the stitches and then use the tail to secure the cord to the left front. Tie a snug knot in the I-cord on the top of the button.

Make pockets, as described in the sidebar on the facing page (optional). Secure all yarn tails. Wash the finished sweater to restore the shape of the garment and to help set the stitches— especially important when working with chunky, heavy yarn. I wash and rinse sweaters by hand, but put them in the washing machine and set if for the spin cycle to eliminate as much water as possible. Then I lay the sweater flat to dry.

Patch Pockets

Patch pockets can be knitted separately and sewn onto a garment. Or you can pick up stitches and work the pockets directly on the garment fronts. The pockets for Chiquita Jacketta were worked 6 stitches from the lower edge and 6 rows from the front edge.

With the right side facing you, pick up 20 stitches by slipping the smaller needle through the right loop of each stitch in that column of stitches (see top photograph at right). I prefer to use the smaller needle to pick up the stitches because it is easier and neater to work than the US 17/12.75 mm needle. Knit the stitches onto the larger needle and continue in stockinette with the MC and the larger needles for 5" (13 cm).

Change to the smaller needles and CC1 to knit the pocket band. Increase stitches in the first row of the band by knitting into every alternate stitch twice, then work the corrugated band for 2 repeats and bind off loosely. Sew the side edges of the pocket to the garment, taking care to line them up squarely.

If you prefer, you can instead knit the sides of the pocket onto the garment while you work by picking up and knitting 1 stitch from the garment at the end of every pocket row. Before you do, however, it is a good idea to baste a contrasting strand of yarn through the rows on the garment to mark the sides of the pocket. Also, stop periodically to check and make sure the pocket and the garment underneath it are smooth and neatly attached. Otherwise, you'll need to unravel the entire pocket to fix any problems you happen to notice later.

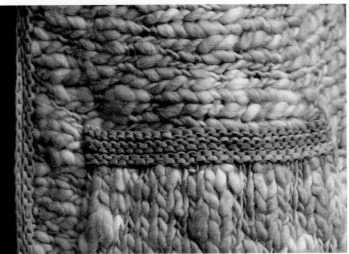

Top Photo: Pick up half of each stitch along the vertical column of stitches that will form the base of the pocket, as shown above. **Bottom Photo:** The finished pocket has an eight-row corrugated band at the top. (The sides of the pockets are marked with contrasting yarn.)

summer twist

A simple, two-row twisted stitch pattern creates a fabulous texture stitch that is easy to knit and that looks a lot like crochet—the perfect detail for this lightweight top with a summery silhouette.

Featured Design Variations

- Short sleeves
- Knitted-on garter stitch bands that form tapered ties
- Two-row twisted stitch

pattern (with a "bump" every two rows that makes it easy to count)

Yarn: Classic Elite "Classic Silk" (135 yards/123 meters per 1.75 ounce/50 gram ball) color #6904, Persian Turquoise, 7 (7, 8, 8, 9, 9) balls

Needles: US 8/5 mm OR SIZE TO OBTAIN GAUGE; for finishing, set of size US 7/4.5 mm double-pointed needles (optional 16"/40 cm size US 7/4.5 mm circular needle for neckband)

Notions: tapestry needle, 2 stitch holders, tape measure

Gauge: 21 stitches and 26 rows = 4" (10 cm) in pattern stitch

Sizes: Women's XS (S, M, L, XL, XXL). *Model is wearing size M.*

Finished Measurements:

Garment width: 17 (18, 20, 22, 24, 26)"/43 (46, 51, 56, 61, 66) cm

Garment length: 18 (18, 18.5, 18.5, 19, 19)"/46 (46, 47, 47, 48, 48) cm

Center back to sleeve edge: 13.5 (14, 15, 16, 17, 18)"/34 (35.5, 38, 41, 43, 46) cm

Stitch Chart

Row 2 (and all even-numbered/right-side rows): *Right twist, purl**, repeat from * to **

Row 1 (and all odd-numbered/wrong-side rows): knit

⊠ Right twist. Knit the 2nd stitch on the left needle. Then knit the 1st stitch on the left needle and drop both stitches from the left needle.

– Purl stitch on the right side; knit stitch on the wrong side.

Step 1

With scrap yarn (see page 19), cast on 66 (66, 72, 72, 76, 76) stitches and knit a couple of rows. Change to MC and, beginning with a knit row, work in pattern until the sleeve measures 5" (13 cm), *at the same time* increasing 1 stitch each end of every other row 3 times and every 4th row 6 times, working at least two rows after the last increase and ending with a pattern row. 84 (84, 90, 90, 94, 94) stitches.

Step 2

With scrap, cast on 53 stitches at each end of the needle and, beginning with a plain knit row, continue working in pattern until the first shoulder measures 5 (5.5, 6.5, 7.25, 8.25, 9)"/13 (14, 16.5, 18.5, 21, 23) cm. Place 95 (95, 98, 98, 100, 100) stitches for the back on a holder (or slide to the end of the needle and do not work these stitches while you knit the front neckline). Note the pattern row.

The second stitch is knitted before the first stitch, and then both stitches are released from the left needle, miraculously crossed.

Step 3

Working only on the front 95 (95, 98, 98, 100, 100) stitches and continuing in pattern, shape the front neckline as follows: Every alternate row, at the neck

edge only, bind off 5 stitches two times, 4 stitches once, 2 stitches once, then 1 stitch twice. 18 stitches decreased. Work straight for 3.5 (3.5, 3.5, 4, 4, 4.5)"/9 (9, 9, 10, 10, 11.5) cm. Then increase, every alternate row, 1 stitch twice, 2 stitches once, 4 stitches once, and 5 stitches twice. Note the pattern row and put the front stitches on a holder (or slide to the end of the needle and do not work these stitches while you knit the front neckline).

Step 4

Return the back stitches to the needle and, resuming patterning, work until the back neck is 7 (7, 7, 7.5, 7.5, 8)"/18 (18, 18, 19, 19, 20.5) cm. Return the front stitches to the needle and work across all the stitches, maintaining pattern, until the second shoulder matches the first, ending with a knit row.

Step 5

At the beginning of the next 2 rows, scrap off 53 stitches (see page 20). 84 (84, 90, 90, 94, 94) stitches remain. Work the second sleeve until it measures 5" (13 cm), *at the same time* decreasing 1 stitch at each end of every 4th row 6 times and every other row 3 times. 66 (66, 72, 72, 76, 76) stitches remain, ending with a knit row. Scrap off.

Finishing

Join the side seams with slip crochet or 3-needle bind-off. Sew the sleeve seams with mattress stitch. The sleeve and lower edges will be finished with knitted-on garter stitch bands (see sidebar on facing page).

For the neckline, with double-pointed needles or short circular needle and beginning at left shoulder, pick up approximately 75 (75, 75, 79, 79, 85) stitches from front and back of garment. Work 3 rows of garter stitch and then bind off loosely. When working garter

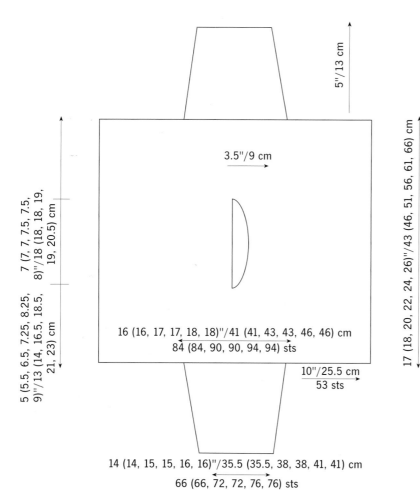

5"/13 cm

3.5"/9 cm

7 (7, 7, 7.5, 7.5, 8)"/18 (18, 18, 19, 19, 20.5) cm

5 (5.5, 6.5, 7.25, 8.25, 9)"/13 (14, 16.5, 18.5, 21, 23) cm

17 (18, 20, 22, 24, 26)"/43 (46, 51, 56, 61, 66) cm

16 (16, 17, 17, 18, 18)"/41 (41, 43, 43, 46, 46) cm
84 (84, 90, 90, 94, 94) sts

10"/25.5 cm
53 sts

14 (14, 15, 15, 16, 16)"/35.5 (35.5, 38, 38, 41, 41) cm
66 (66, 72, 72, 76, 76) sts

stitch in the round, you must alternate knit and purl rounds, beginning with a purl round.

To work the sleeve bands, begin and end picking up the live stitches at the center of the sleeve so that the ties are on top. Double every 6th stitch by knitting 2 stitches together to slightly taper the lower edge of the sleeve.

For the lower edge of the garment, pick up approximately 60 (60, 74, 84, 94, 100) stitches (about 1 stitch per "bump") on the front to work the garter stitch band bind-off, and then repeat for the back.

Work in all yarn tails. Wash the sweater and dry to shape. Tie ends in soft knots at side seams and sleeves.

Garter Stitch Bands with Tie Extensions

The directions for the lower bands appear first. The directions for the sleeve bands are in parentheses. Knit all rows.

Knitting the beginning tie:

With a pair of double-pointed needles, cast on 2 stitches. *Knit 2 rows, increase 1 stitch at the beginning of the next row.** Repeat from * to ** until there are 10 (7) stitches.

Work 6 (4) rows straight.

Decrease 1 stitch at each end of the next and following alternate rows 2 (1) times until 6 (5) stitches remain. Knit 10 rows straight.

Attaching the band to the garment edge:

With a separate strand of yarn (so you can pick up from right to left) and the right side facing, pick up the garment edge with a needle long enough to accommodate all of the stitches and hold the needle in the left hand. (For the sleeves, use a short circular needle or the remaining 3 double-pointed needles). Cut the yarn.

Position the double-pointed needle holding the tie so that you will be able to work as follows to attach the band to the garment as you work: *With wrong side facing, knit 1 row across band stitches. Knit 5 (4). Slip last stitch to the left needle, which holds the garment edge stitches. Knit 2 together from the left needle.** Repeat from * to ** across garment edge until all stitches have been worked from the left needle. You'll develop a rhythm for turning the double-pointed needle back and forth to knit each row without turning the whole garment.

Join the band to the edge of the sweater by knitting two stitches together every alternate row—the last one from the band and the next one from the edge of the sweater (shown on the pink needle).

Knitting the ending tie:

Work 10 rows straight on the band stitches, then increase 1 stitch at each end of the next and following alternate rows 2 (1) times until there are 10 (7) stitches. Knit 6 (4) rows straight.

Decrease 1 stitch at the end of every alternate row until 2 stitches remain. Knit those 2 stitches together and draw yarn through the loop to secure.

jewels

Simple shaping makes this little tied shrug easy to knit. Delicious yarns and generous ties make it fun to wear!

Featured Design Variations

- Simple back neckline (barely a slit, with no shaping at all)
- Fronts that extend to form self-ties
- Single crochet edge finish
- Three-color garter stitch variation with "slides"

Yarns: Collezione S. Charles "Ritratto" (28% mohair, 53% rayon, 10% polyamide, 9% polyester with 198 yards/180 meters per 1.75 ounce/50 gram ball), CC1 color #64, 3 (3, 3, 4, 4, 4) balls; "Rialto" (57% polyester, 35% rayon, 6% acrylic, 2% polyamide with 65 yards/60 meters per 1.75 ounce/50 gram ball), CC2 color #24, 4 (4, 4, 5, 5, 5) balls; "Cosmos" (45% rayon, 40% polyamide, 15% cotton with 87 yards/80 meters per 1.75 ounce/ 50 gram ball), CC3 color #1123, 3 (3, 3, 4, 4, 4) balls

Needles: Size US 7/4.5 mm circular needle (29"/80 cm) OR SIZE TO OBTAIN GAUGE

Notions: tape measure, yarn bras (to avoid slippery yarns spilling), crochet hook size US D/3.25 mm

Gauge: 18 stitches and 38 rows = 4" (10 cm)

Sizes: Women's XS (S, M, L, XL, XXL).

Model is wearing size M.

Finished Measurements:

Garment width: 18 (20, 22, 24, 25, 26)"/ 46 (51, 56, 61, 63.5, 66) cm

Garment length: 17 (17, 18, 18, 19, 19)"/ 43 (43, 46, 46, 48, 48) cm

Center back to sleeve edge: 26 (27, 28, 29, 29.5, 30)"/66 (69, 71, 74, 75, 76) cm

Note:

Slip one of the stretchy yarn bras over each ball of yarn to prevent the yarn from spilling out of control. These little nets stretch to fit snugly, and you may need to help the yarn feed as you work.

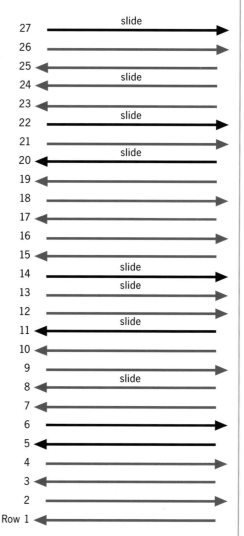

Color Order Chart

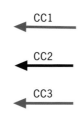

CC1

CC2

CC3

Knit all rows. When the directions indicate "slide," literally slide the work to the other end of the needle to begin working from the other end of the row (instead of turning the work, as usual). This process will introduce stockinette stitch between the ridges of garter stitch. To execute the slides, you need a circular needle or long double-pointed needles.

The three yarns are indicated as CC1 (Ritratto), CC2 (Rialto), and CC3 (Venus). The 27-row color order repeats throughout the sweater.

Try to twist or cross the yarns at the edges as you work them in order to bind them to the edge of the garment.

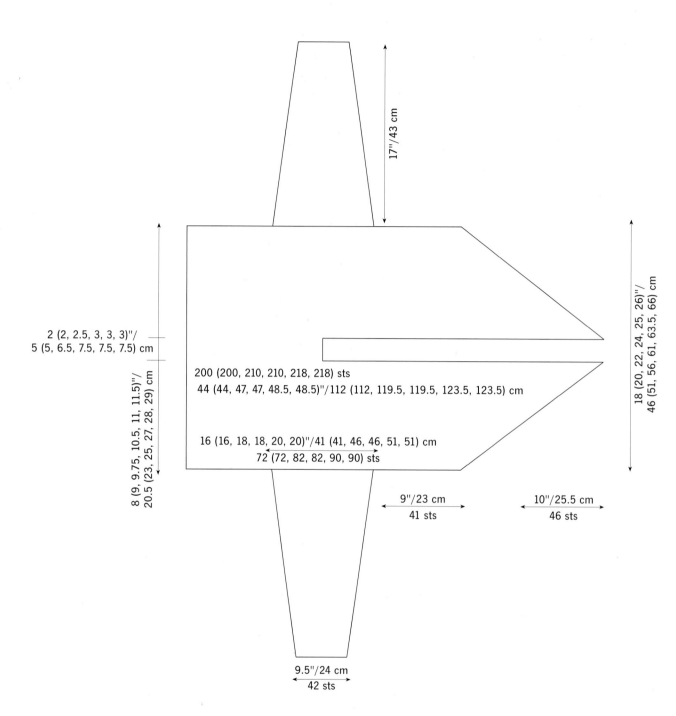

17"/43 cm

2 (2, 2.5, 3, 3, 3)"/
5 (5, 6.5, 7.5, 7.5, 7.5) cm

8 (9, 9.75, 10.5, 11, 11.5)"/
20.5 (23, 25, 27, 28, 29) cm

18 (20, 22, 24, 25, 26)"/
46 (51, 56, 61, 63.5, 66) cm

200 (200, 210, 210, 218, 218) sts
44 (44, 47, 47, 48.5, 48.5)"/112 (112, 119.5, 119.5, 123.5, 123.5) cm

16 (16, 18, 18, 20, 20)"/41 (41, 46, 46, 51, 51) cm
72 (72, 82, 82, 90, 90) sts

9"/23 cm
41 sts

10"/25.5 cm
46 sts

9.5"/24 cm
42 sts

17 (17, 18, 18, 19, 19)"/43 (43, 46, 46, 48, 48) cm

Step 1

With size 7/4.5 mm needles and scrap yarn (see page 17), cast on 42 stitches and knit a couple of rows. Change to CC1 to begin working the color order for 17" (43 cm), *at the same time* increase 1 stitch each end every 6th row 0 (0, 0, 0, 12, 12) times, every 8th row 0 (0, 16, 16, 12, 12) times, every 10th row 6 (6, 4, 4, 0, 0) times, and every 12th row 9 (9, 0, 0, 0, 0) times. 72 (72, 82, 82, 90, 90) stitches. Work all increases 1 stitch from the edge to facilitate seaming later on.

Step 2

Cut all three CC yarns. Scrap on 41 stitches at each end of the needle. Reattach yarns at the lower back edge to continue the color order with all 3 yarns over the entire 154 (154, 164, 164, 172, 172) stitches and immediately begin shaping the right front tie by increasing 1 stitch (at the lower front end of) every other row 30 (38, 46, 42, 40, 38) times, then 2 stitches every other row 8 (4, 0, 0, 0, 0) times, then 1 stitch every 4th row 0 (0, 0, 4, 6, 8) times until there are 200 (200, 210, 210, 218, 218) stitches.

Step 3

Scrap off the 123 (123, 128, 128, 132, 132) front stitches and continue working on the 77 (77, 82, 82, 86, 86) back stitches alone for 2 (2, 2.5, 3, 3, 3)"/5 (5, 6.5, 7.5, 7.5, 7.5) cm.

Step 4

Keep the back stitches on the needle. Scrap on 123 (123, 128, 128, 132, 132) stitches for the left front, knit several rows, then cut the scrap. Continue working these front stitches along with the back stitches to shape the second side of the body. Immediately begin shaping the lower front edge by decreasing 1 stitch every 4th row 0 (0, 0, 4, 6, 8) times, then 2 stitches every other row 8 (4, 0, 0, 0, 0) times, then 1 stitch every other row 30 (38, 46, 42, 40, 38) times until 154 (154, 164, 164, 172, 172) stitches remain.

Step 5

Scrap off 41 stitches at each end of the needle (see page 20) and continue on the remaining 72 (72, 82, 82, 90, 90) stitches until sleeve measures 17" (43 cm), *at the same time* decreasing 1 stitch each end of every 12th row 9 (9, 0, 0, 0, 0) times, every 10th row 6 (6, 4, 4, 0, 0) times, every 8th row 0 (0, 16, 16, 12, 12) times, and every 6th row 0 (0, 0, 0, 12, 12) times. Scrap off remaining 42 stitches.

Finishing

Seam the sides of the jacket with slip crochet (see page 25) or three-needle bind-off (see page 91) and sew the sleeve seams with mattress stitch (see page 22). Fold back the scrap yarn at the edge of the sleeve and, with the right side facing you and CC2, work 1 row of single crochet, as shown in the drawings on page 25. Repeat for the second sleeve. Then work one continuous row around the lower and neckline edges of the jacket. Work in all yarn tails and remove any scrap knitting. Wash the finished shrug and lay flat to shape.

classic stripes

This garter stitch fabric looks great on both the right and the "wrong" sides, giving you the option of having a garment with crisp, colorful stripes or one with muted shading.

Featured Design Variations

- Easy-to-knit garter stitch (knit every row)
- Stripes extend to create decorative color tabs at garment hem
- Square neckline with fast and easy shaping
- Self-finished garter stitch edges
- Crochet finish on garter stitch neckline band

Yarn: Tahki "Cotton Classic" (100% mercerized cotton with 108 yards/100 meters per 1.75 ounces/50 grams), 1 (1, 2, 2, 2, 3) skeins each of #420 Tweedy Cotton for MC, #3772 Aqua (CC1), #3942 Purple (CC2), #3815 Turquoise (CC3), and 1 (1, 1, 1, 2, 2) skeins #3873 Blue (CC4)

Needles: US size 4/3.5 mm circular needle (16"/40 cm) and US size 6/4 mm OR SIZE TO OBTAIN GAUGE

Notions: tapestry needle, 2 stitch holders, tape measure, clip clothespin, US size D/3.25 mm crochet hook

Gauge: 20 stitches and 42 rows = 4" (10 cm) in garter stitch (after washing)

Sizes: Children's 2 (4, 6, 8, 10, 12). *Model is wearing size 6.*

Finished Measurements:

Garment width: 12 (13, 14, 15, 16, 17)"/30.5 (33, 35.5, 38, 41, 43) cm

Garment length (not including tabs): 10 (12, 14, 16, 17.5, 20)"/25.5 30.5, 35.5, 41, 44.5, 51) cm

Center back to sleeve cuff: 15 (16.5, 18, 19.5, 21, 22.5)"/38 (42, 46, 50, 53, 57) cm

Notes:

Begin every row by slipping the first stitch as if to knit. Knit the second stitch and then give the yarn a little tug to tighten up the edge stitch. When knitting the first row of a new color, do *not* slip the first stitch.

All of the stripes are knitted with an even number of rows, and the stripe order is nonrepeating. The charts indicate row-by-row color for each size.

Each row on the charts represents *two* knitted rows, but each square represents just one stitch. Beginning rows are indicated for each size so that there isn't an awkward two-row stripe disturbing the flow of the others. The sleeve chart indicates one row of CC3/turquoise with an asterisk (*) that needs to be knitted in CC4/blue instead *for size 6 only*.

Always change colors on a right-side row so that the garment has consistently solid color stripes on one side and muted stripes on the other. Do not carry colors along the edges because the strands will show.

To keep the stitches from loosening when ending/starting colors, hold the ends securely with a clip clothespin until the new color is established. You can also knit one stitch with the new color, then hold the tail of the new color with the working end, use both strands to knit the next stitch, and then drop the tail. This process will secure the new color and won't be noticeable. The end will still need to be worked in later, but this will help maintain tension while you knit.

If you prefer to weave in the ends as you knit (see page 77), pay close attention to the right and wrong sides of the fabric. Work in the ends at the lower sleeve after the sweater is assembled in case you need/want to turn back a cuff.

Hand-wash and machine-dry the swatch before measuring to ensure the correct final gauge for the garment.

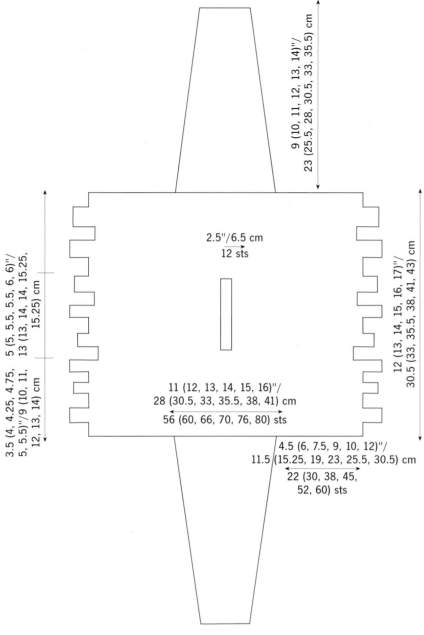

9 (10, 11, 12, 13, 14)"/
23 (25.5, 28, 30.5, 33, 35.5) cm

2.5"/6.5 cm
12 sts

5 (5, 5.5, 5.5, 6, 6)"/
13 (13, 14, 14, 15.25, 15.25) cm

3.5 (4, 4.25, 4.75, 5, 5.5)"/9 (10, 11, 12, 13, 14) cm

11 (12, 13, 14, 15, 16)"/
28 (30.5, 33, 35.5, 38, 41) cm
56 (60, 66, 70, 76, 80) sts

12 (13, 14, 15, 16, 17)"/
30.5 (33, 35.5, 38, 41, 43) cm

4.5 (6, 7.5, 9, 10, 12)"/
11.5 (15.25, 19, 23, 25.5, 30.5) cm
22 (30, 38, 45,
52, 60) sts

6 (6, 6, 6.5, 6.5, 6.5)"/15.25 (15.25, 15.25, 16, 16, 16) cm
30 (30, 30, 32, 32, 32) sts

Step 1

Consult the sleeve chart for the first row for each size and then scrap on (see page 19) or, using the color shown, cast on 30 (30, 30, 32, 32, 32) stitches. Follow the stripe order shown on the chart, always changing color on a right side row, *at the same time* increasing 1 stitch each end of every 8th row 10 (9, 5, 5, 3, 2) times, then every 6th row 3 (6, 13, 14, 19, 22) times until the sleeve measures 9 (10, 11, 12, 13, 14)"/23 (25.5, 28, 30.5, 33, 35.5) cm. 56 (60, 66, 70, 76, 80) stitches. Place a marker at the center stitch. The marker will slip from needle to needle as you work the following rows. (Note that the single row indicated for a color change is for size 6 only.)

Step 2

At the end of the next two rows, cast on 22 (30, 38, 45, 52, 60) stitches and follow the stripe chart for the body until 3.5 (4, 4.25, 4.75, 5, 5.5)"/9 (10, 11, 12, 13, 14) cm have been knitted for the right shoulder, *at the same time* begin increasing and decreasing to form the hemline tabs as shown on the chart. When the first shoulder is complete, put all of the stitches to the left of the marker onto a stitch holder for the back.

Step 3

Working on the front stitches only, bind off 12 stitches at the neck, and then work straight, shaping hemline tabs, until the neck measures 5 (5, 5.5, 5.5, 6, 6)"/13 (13, 14, 14, 15, 15) cm. Cast on 12 stitches at the neck edge and then put all of the front stitches on a holder.

Step 4

Return the back stitches to the needle and work the back to match the front, omitting neckline shaping, then return the front stitches to the needle and

Sleeve Chart

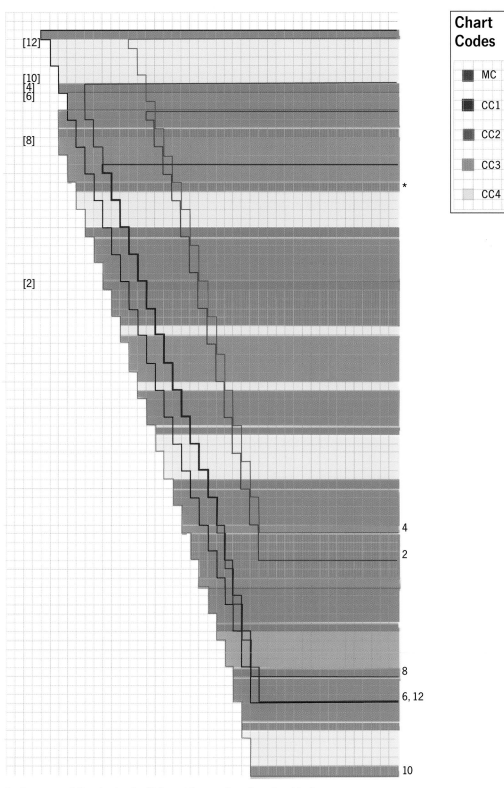

Chart Codes

- MC
- CC1
- CC2
- CC3
- CC4

Each square of the chart = 1 stitch and 2 rows (i.e., 1 garter ridge).

Numbers shown in [brackets] refer to starting rows for second sleeve, worked from the top down.

* For size 6 only, knit this stripe as CC1.

Body Chart

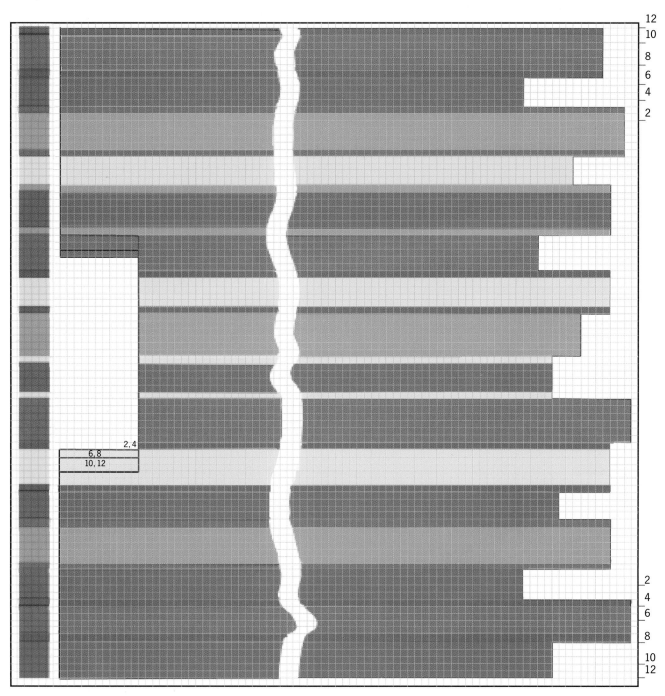

work across all stitches, shaping hemline tabs, until the second shoulder matches the first.

Step 5

At the beginning of the next 2 rows, scrap off/bind off 22 (30, 38, 45, 52, 60) stitches so that only 56 (60, 66, 70, 76, 80) stitches remain for the sleeve. Work the second sleeve by following the chart from the top down, beginning where indicated on the chart for each size, *at the same time* decreasing 1 stitch at each end of every 6th row 3 (6, 13, 14, 19, 22) times, then every 8th row 10 (9, 5, 5, 3, 2) times. 30 (30, 30, 32, 32, 32) stitches remain. Bind off loosely.

Finishing

Sew the side and sleeve seams. If turning back a sleeve cuff, reverse the sleeve seam so it does not show when the cuff is turned, and work in those tails *on the right side*. With right side facing you, smaller needle, MC, and beginning at left shoulder, pick up approximately 12 stitches along side of neckline, 30 (30, 33, 33, 36, 36) stitches across front, 12 stitches along second side, and 30 (30, 33, 33, 36, 36) stitches along back. Purl the first round, decreasing 6 stitches evenly across the back and 6 stitches across the front by purling 2 stitches together. Then work 10 rows/5 garter ridges by knitting one round, purling one round, *at the same time* decreasing 1 stitch at each front corner on every knit round by knitting 2 stitches together. Bind off as loosely as possible.

With CC4 and the wrong side facing you, work 1 row of single crochet through the inner half of each bound-off stitch. Work in all yarn tails. Hand-wash and machine-dry the finished sweater to help set the stitches, size the sweater, and secure the yarn tails.

Colored Tabs

All of the tabs are shaped by increasing and decreasing stitches, as shown on the chart on the facing page. Most of the tabs are outlined with two rows of another color. All of the increases must be done with the simple looped cast-on (see page 90). Although this cast-on seems loose and unstructured while you are doing it, the edge works perfectly with garter stitch, neither binding the stitches too tightly nor lacking shape. None of the other cast-ons will work without adding extra partial rows of a color or ending up with awkward gaps mid-tab.

Work a couple of tabs on your swatch to get comfortable with the method described here. The front and back tabs are knitted exactly the same and, when working the shoulder sections, they are knitted at the same time.

To illustrate the technique, let's assume that the first tab you knit has a blue edge on either side of a purple stripe. When you reach the tab, cast 11 stitches onto the right needle with blue and *keep these stitches on the right needle*. Continue knitting across all the stitches on the left needle (with the blue) and then cast on 11 stitches at the end of the row for the corresponding back tab. Knit back across all of the stitches (back tab, back, front, front tab) and then cut the blue. Work the next 4 rows across all of the stitches with the purple, then 1 row with blue. At the beginning of the second blue row, bind off 15 stitches, knit across to the other end of the row, and bind off the last 15 stitches. Work the next 4 rows with the tweed yarn (for example) and then begin the next tab.

When binding off, just use a basic bind-off, knitting 2 stitches, then passing the first stitch over the second. Knit 1 stitch and repeat until you have bound off the required number of stitches.

autumn leaves

The striped ribs on this V-neck cardigan accentuate the rich, hand-dyed colors of the main yarn. This is the perfect garment for a crisp fall day!

Featured Design Variations

- Cardigan style
- V-neckline with short-row shaping
- Striped bands, worked in k2p2 ribbing

- All-over texture stitch, to accentuate the coloration of the yarn
- Shawl collar (optional)
- Patch pockets (optional)

Yarn: Manos del Uruguay (100% wool with approximately 138 yards/151 meters per 3.5 ounce/100 gram skein), MC color #109 Woodland, 7 (7, 8, 8, 9, 9) skeins, and 1 skein each CC1 color #35 Uranium, CC2 color #55 Olive, and CC3 color V Cinnamon; 1 ball cotton or nonfuzzy acrylic yarn for scrap knitting

Gauge: 16 stitches and 21 rows = 4" (10 cm) in pattern stitch

Needles: Size US 7/4.5 mm and US 9/5.5 mm needles OR SIZE TO OBTAIN GAUGE; optional size 7/4.5 mm double-pointed needles for sleeve ribs

Notions: tapestry needle, row counter (optional), 5 buttons

Sizes: Women's XS (S, M, L, XL, XXL). *Model is wearing size M.*

Finished Measurements:

Garment width: 18 (20, 22, 24, 26, 28)"/46 (51, 56, 61, 66, 71) cm

Garment length: 24 (24.5, 25, 25.5, 26, 26)"/61 (62, 63.5, 65, 66, 66) cm

Center back to sleeve (not including rib): 25 (26, 27, 28, 29, 30)"/63.5 (66, 69, 71, 74, 76) cm

Stitch Chart

Edge stitch

8-row repeat

4-stitch repeat

☐ (Yarn over, knit 1) twice. Pass the 2nd yarn-over over the second knit-1, then pass the first yarn-over over both knit-1 stitches.

☐ Knit stitch on the right side; purl stitch on the wrong side

Notes:

According to personal preference, you can shape the V-neckline conventionally with decreasing rather than with short rows.

Start and end all sections with a few rows of scrap knitting, rather than a conventional cast-on or bind-off, to ensure that both sleeves are bound off the same way and that there are live stitches to graft the side seams. Grafting will reduce the bulk substantially and streamline the fit. Scrap knitting retains live stitches along both front edges, too.

The sleeve ribs are knitted last so that you can check that their bound-off edges are identical when folded back. Try on the jacket and alter the sleeve length if necessary.

See page 17 for detail of stitch pattern.

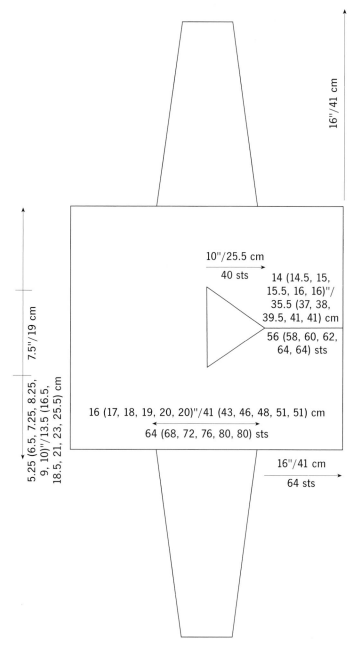

10"/25.5 cm
40 sts

16"/41 cm

14 (14.5, 15, 15.5, 16, 16)"/ 35.5 (37, 38, 39.5, 41, 41) cm

56 (58, 60, 62, 64, 64) sts

7.5"/19 cm

5.25 (6.5, 7.25, 8.25, 9, 10)"/13.5 (16.5, 18.5, 21, 23, 25.5) cm

16 (17, 18, 19, 20, 20)"/41 (43, 46, 48, 51, 51) cm
64 (68, 72, 76, 80, 80) sts

18 (20, 22, 24, 26, 28)"/46 (51, 56, 61, 66, 71) cm

16"/41 cm
64 sts

9 (9, 9, 9.5, 10, 10.5)"/23 (23, 23, 24, 25.5, 27) cm
36 (36, 36, 38, 40, 42) sts

(Yarn over, knit 1) twice. Pass the second yarn-over over the second knit-1.

Then pass the first yarn-over over both of the knit-1 stitches. The yarn-overs will encircle the two knit stitches.

Step 1

With the larger needles and scrap yarn, cast on 36 (36, 36, 38, 40, 42) stitches and knit a couple of rows (see page 19). Change to the MC and work in pattern until the sleeve measures 16" (41 cm) from the beginning. *At the same time,* increase 1 stitch each end of every 8th row 0 (0, 3, 0, 0, 0) times, every 7th row 0 (2, 0, 0, 0, 0) times, every 6th row 14 (0, 0, 3, 2, 3) times, every 5th row 0 (14, 0, 2, 0, 2) times, and every 4th row 0 (0, 15, 14, 18, 14) times. Incorporate the increased stitches into the pattern as soon as you can, always maintaining a plain edge stitch. 64 (68, 72, 76, 80, 80) stitches, ending with a wrong side row.

Cut the main yarn and push the sleeve stitches to the center of the needle. Make a note of the pattern row. With scrap yarn, cast on 64 stitches at one end of the needle and knit a couple of rows, ending with a wrong side row as for the sleeve. Repeat the scrap at the other end of the needle so that there are now 192 (196, 200, 204, 208, 208) stitches.

Step 2

Reattach the main yarn (MC) at the end of the needle and knit (without pattern) across the first scrap section, pattern the sleeve stitches, and knit the second scrap section. Then pattern across all stitches for 5.25 (6.5, 7.5, 8.25, 9, 10)"/13.5 (16.5, 19, 21, 23, 25.5) cm, ending with a wrong side row at the lower front edge. Place the 96 (98, 100, 102, 104, 104) stitches for the back on a holder to begin the right front neck shaping. Make a note of the pattern row.

Step 3

Maintaining the stitch patterning, short row 4 stitches every other row 10 times as follows: Knit to the last 4 stitches on the needle (at the neck edge), wrap, turn, and purl back. Next row and all following right-side rows, work 4 fewer stitches until 40 stitches have been short-rowed (see page 85), 20 rows knitted, and 56 (58, 60, 62, 64, 64) stitches remain active. Place a marker to indicate the beginning of the neck shaping after the last short row.

Knit (*not* in pattern) the next (right side) row across *all* 96 (98, 100, 102, 104, 104) stitches, taking care to knit the wraps with the wrapped stitches. At the neck edge, replace the back stitches on the needle and work across them to the end of the row, *taking care to continue the patterning on the back where it left off when you removed the back stitches to the holder*. Make a note of the pattern row for the front and then knit 3 rows of scrap across all the front stitches and bind off loosely. Resume the stitch patterning to knit the back stitches alone for 40 rows and then place them on a stitch holder.

Step 4

With scrap, cast on 96 (98, 100, 102, 104, 104) stitches and knit a few rows.

Change to the MC and purl 1 row across all stitches, ending the row at the lower front edge. Continue the stitch pattern from the row where it ended on the right front and begin increasing by short rows as follows: Work across 56 (58, 60, 62, 64, 64) stitches (place a yarn marker to indicate the beginning of the neck shaping), wrap, turn, and purl back.

Next row and all following right side rows, work 4 more stitches each row until all 96 (98, 100, 102, 104, 104) stitches are active.

Return the back stitches to the needle and work across all 192 (196, 200, 204, 208, 208) stitches until the second shoulder matches the first. When the back stitches are returned to the needle, the pattern should be continuous and correct from front to back. If not, add or subtract a row from the front or back until it is.

Step 5

In preparation for knitting the second sleeve and to end with a plain knit (not patterned) row to facilitate seaming, knit the first 64 stitches, pattern the next 64 (68, 72, 76, 80, 80) stitches, and knit the last 64 stitches. Cut the main yarn.

With scrap, knit several rows across the first 64 stitches. Bind off these stitches and then repeat at the other end of the needle so that only the center 64 (68, 72, 76, 80, 80) stitches remain. Knit the sleeve until it measures 16" (41 cm) from the shoulder, *at the same time* decreasing 1 stitch each end of every 4th row 0 (0, 15, 14, 18, 14) times, every 5th row 0 (14, 0, 2, 0, 2) times, every 6th row 14 (0, 0, 3, 2, 3) times, every 7th row 0 (2, 0, 0, 0, 0) times, then every 8th row 0 (0, 3, 0, 0, 0) times. 36 (36, 36, 38, 40, 42) stitches remain. Work several rows of scrap and bind off.

Finishing

Block the garment piece. Press the scrap knitting (but not the sweater) so it lies flat. With the smaller needle and the right side of the garment facing you, fold back the scrap knitting and pick up the sleeve stitches. Work k2p2 rib for 18 rows as follows: (1 row each CC1, CC2, and CC3) six times. Bind off with a strand of the MC and leave a long enough tail to use for seaming the sleeve. Remove the scrap. Repeat for the second sleeve. This cuff will be deep enough to turn back.

Sew the sleeve seams, reversing the cuff seam so that it is on the *outside* of the sweater but will not show on the cuff itself when folded back. For a narrower cuff that does not fold back, knit only 9 to 12 rows and do not reverse the seam. (Alternatively, you could sew the sleeve seam first and then use double-pointed needles to knit the turn-back ribbing, avoiding the seam altogether.)

Working 1 row each of three colors will create a rotation where each color will always be in the right place if you start correctly. Work CC1 from right to left, CC2 from left to right, and CC3 from right to left. CC1 will be waiting to knit the next row from left to right.

Graft the side seams (see page 23) and then remove the scrap knitting.

With the smaller needle and the right side facing, pick up *approximately* 126 (142, 154, 170, 182, 194) stitches evenly around the lower edge. Work k2p2 rib for 6 rows as for the sleeves.

With the smaller needle and the right side facing you, fold back the scrap knitting to pick up 4 stitches along bottom right ribbing, the right front stitches from the scrap knitting, 38 stitches across the back neckline, then the left front stitches from the scrap knitting, and 4 stitches along bottom left ribbing. 238 (242, 246, 250, 258, 258) stitches.

For a simple ribbed band, work 6 rows k2p2 rib as for the lower edge, making 5 two-stitch buttonholes on the right front band in the 3rd row. Buttonholes should start 4 (2, 4, 2, 2, 2) stitches from the lower edge, with 11 (12, 12, 13, 14, 14) stitches between each one (see facing page). The last buttonhole should be close to the start of the neckline shaping. Work in all yarn tails and sew buttons to the left front under the buttonholes.

Design Options

Shawl Collar For the optional shawl collar, follow the same color order as for the other bands and work the collar in k2p2 rib. Beginning at the lower right front edge, pick up 238 (242, 246, 250, 258, 258) stitches as shown in the drawing, placing markers at "A" and "B" and at the base of the V-neck on each front.

Knit from the lower left front to "A," wrap, turn, and knit to "B." Wrap, turn, and knit 2 stitches beyond "A." ★Wrap, turn, and knit 2 more stitches than previous row.★★ Repeat from ★ to ★★, working 2 more stitches at the end of

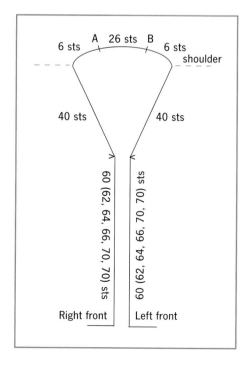

every row, until the knitting reaches the markers at the base of the V-neckline.

Work 1 row over entire right front edge. Work the next 2 rows over all 238 (242, 246, 250, 258, 258) stitches, knitting any wraps with the wrapped stitches, and making 5 evenly spaced buttonholes in the third row. Work 3 more rows over all stitches and bind off loosely with the MC.

Pockets To position the pockets, try on the sweater. Pin 5" x 6" (13 x 15.25 cm) paper "pockets" to the fronts to see at what height you can easily slip your hands into the pockets. The pockets should be 3.5 (3.5, 4, 4, 4.5, 4.5)"/9

(9, 10, 10, 11.5, 11.5) cm from the front edge of the sweater.

With the right side facing up and with the larger needles and the MC, pick up 22 stitches from the surface of the sweater for the lower edge of the pocket (see page 24). Purl back and then work in pattern for 5" (13 cm). Change to the smaller needles and work 6 rows k2p2 rib as before. With the MC and a tapestry needle, neatly sew the sides of the pockets to the sweater fronts. (Alternatively, the pockets can be knitted right onto the sweater by picking up half a stitch from every other row of the garment to knit with the edge pocket stitches.)

One-Row Buttonholes

Buttonholes can be worked in several ways, but I use a simple, one-row method. Buttonhole spacing is simple to work out if you remember that there are more spaces between, before, and after the buttons than there are buttons. So, if you plan to have three buttons, you need to plan for two equal spaces between the buttons and then two smaller spaces before the first and after the last button.

The first and last buttons on most cardigans are just a few stitches from the edge, and those spaces can often accommodate any extra rows left over from spacing the other buttons. On V-neck cardigans, the top button is generally even with the beginning of the V-neck shaping. When you knit the button band before you knit the buttonhole band, you can easily count out the rows or ribs and place safety pins where you think the buttons should go. For a continuous band like this one, you have to count the ribs and spacing on the first few rows of the band.

Remember that in addition to the spaces between them, each buttonhole will require 2 to 3 stitches for the buttonhole itself. Always work up a sample so you know exactly how many stitches you'll need to use to create a buttonhole that will be large enough for your button to pass through and snug enough to hold it.

1. Knit to the beginning of the buttonhole and then bring the yarn to the front to slip the first stitch as if to purl then put the yarn in back. (Slip 1, pass the first stitch over the second) two or three times, depending on the size of your button. Return the last stitch from the right needle to the left. Do not turn the work.

2. With the yarn in back, use the cable cast-on method to cast on one more stitch than you bound off in Step 1. Turn the work.

3. With the yarn in back, slip the first stitch from the left needle to the right needle and then pass the last cast-on stitch over it. Continue working to the end of the row or up to the next buttonhole.

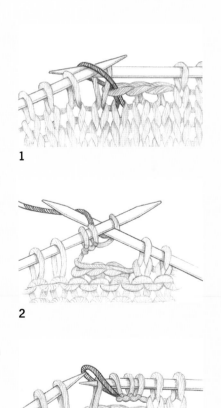

1

2

3

corn and cables

Twisted stitches and popcorn accentuate the cables that run horizontally across this textured pullover. The square neckline is identically shaped in front and back.

Featured Design Variations

- Lower edge has a self-rolled hem
- Sleeve and neck edges finished with narrow I-cord

- Twisted stitches, popcorn stitch, and four-stitch cables on a background of reverse stockinette (the right side is purl)

Yarn: Simply Shetland's "Jamieson's Double Knitting" (100% Shetland wool with 68 yards/75 meters per .88 ounce/25 gram skein), color #230 Yellow Ochre, 13 (14, 16, 18, 20, 21) skeins

Needle: Size US 5/3.75 mm OR SIZE TO OBTAIN GAUGE

Notions: cable needle, 2 stitch holders, tapestry needle, tape measure

Gauge: 24 stitches and 31 rows = 4" (10 cm) over cable pattern

Sizes: Women's XS (S, M, L, XL, XXL). *Model is wearing size M.*

Finished Measurements:

Garment width: 17 (18, 20, 22, 24, 26)"/43 (46, 51, 56, 61, 66) cm

Garment length: 20 (20.5, 21, 21.5, 22, 22)"/51 (52, 53, 55, 56, 56) cm

Center back to sleeve cuff: 25.5 (26, 27, 28, 29, 30)"/65 (66, 69, 71, 74, 76) cm

Step 1

Cast on/scrap on 54 (54, 54, 58, 58, 58) stitches and follow the sleeve chart for cable pattern, increasing 1 stitch each end of every 6th row 21 (17, 9, 9, 2, 2) times, then every 4th row 0 (7, 18, 19, 29, 29) times until the sleeve measures 17" (43 cm) and there are 96 (102, 108, 114, 120, 120) stitches, ending with the pattern row indicated on the chart. *At the same time* incorporate newly increased stitches into pattern as indicated on chart.

Step 2

At the beginning of the next two rows, cast on/scrap on 72 stitches at each end of the row for the front and back. Continuing the cable patterns from the sleeves and beginning the patterns on the appropriate row for the size you are knitting (see charts at right), work until the shoulder measures 5 (5.5, 6.5, 7.5, 8.5, 9.5)"/13 (14, 16.5, 19, 21.5, 24) cm, ending as indicated on chart. Put the 120 (123, 126, 129, 132, 132) back stitches on a holder and note the pattern row to continue later.

Step 3

Begin shaping the front neck by binding off on alternate rows at the neck edge, 7 stitches once, 2 stitches once, then 1 stitch twice. Continue working the front for 5" (13 cm) without further shaping. Note that the chart shows one-half of the neck opening—work the other half over the same number of rows. Shape the second side of the neckline by increasing 1 stitch twice, 2 stitches once, then 7 stitches once. Make a note of the pattern row and put the front stitches on a holder.

Step 4

Return the back stitches to the needle and, continuing pattern, shape the back neckline exactly like the front neckline. When the back matches the front, return the front stitches to the needle, working across all 240 (246, 252, 258, 264, 264) stitches. Begin working the central sleeve cable patterns *in reverse* at the neckline and continue working all of the patterns until the second shoulder matches the first.

Cable Chart Symbols

YF = yarn in front   **YB** = yarn in back   **LN** = left needle   **RN** = right needle   **CN** = cable needle

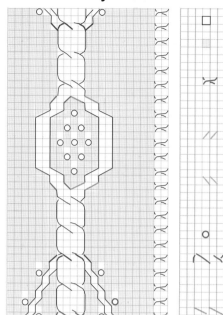

☐ Knit stitch on the right side; purl stitch on the wrong side

▨ Purl stitch on the right side; knit stitch on the wrong side

Right Twist, knit over knit: skip first stitch on LN. Knit *second* stitch, then knit first stitch. Slip both stitches from LN. Can also be worked (more slowly) as 1 x 1 cable by removing first stitch on CN and holding at back. Knit next stitch on LN then knit stitch from CN.

Right Twist, knit over purl: With YB, knit the second stitch on LN. Bring YF to purl first stitch. Slip both stitches off LN. Can also be worked as 1 x 1 cable by slipping first stitch to CN and holding at back. Knit next stitch, then purl stitch from CN (traveling stitches).

Left Twist, knit over purl: With YF, pass the tip of RN behind the first stitch on the LN. Catch right side of second stitch and bring to the front to purl. Put YB and knit first stitch on LN. Slip both stitches from the LN. Can also be worked as 1 x 1 cable: Slip first stitch to CN and hold at front. Purl stitch from LN then knit stitch from CN (traveling stitches).

○ Popcorn

2 x 2 Left Twist Cable: slip first 2 stitches to CN and hold in front. Knit next 2 stitches from LN, then knit 2 stitches from CN.

2 x 2 Left Twist Cable, knits over purls: Slip 2 stitches to CN and hold in front. Purl next 2 stitches from LN. Knit the 2 stitches from CN.

2 x 2 Right Twist Cable, knits over purls: slip first 2 stitches to CN and hold in back. Knit next 2 stitches from LN and then purl 2 from CN.

2 x 1 Left Twist Cable, knits over purls: Slip first 2 stitches to CN and hold in front. Purl next stitch from LN, then knit the 2 stitches from CN (traveling cables).

2 x 1 Right Twist Cable, knits over purls: Slip first stitch to CN and hold in back. Knit next two stitches from LN, then purl the stitch on the CN (traveling cables).

Complex 2 x 2 Left Twist Cable (increases cable from 4 to 6 stitches wide at the crossing): With YB, slip the first stitch to the RN. Slip the next 4 stitches to the CN and hold in front. Slip the first stitch back from the RN to the LN. With YB, return the last 2 stitches from the CN to the LN. Knit 4 stitches from the LN, then the 2 stitches from the CN.

Complex 2 x 2 Left Twist Cable (decreases cable from 6 to 4 stitches wide at the crossing): Slip the first 2 stitches to the CN and hold in front. Purl 1 stitch from the LN and slip the next stitch to the RN. Slip the next 2 stitches to the CN and hold in front. Return 1 stitch from the RN to the LN. Return the last 2 stitches from the CN to the LN. Knit 2 stitches from the LN, knit 2 stitches from the CN, and purl 1 stitch from the LN.

Step 5

At the beginning of the next two rows, bind off/scrap off 72 stitches and continue working the patterns down the sleeve, *at the same time* decreasing 1 stitch each end of every 4th row 0 (7, 18, 19, 29, 29) times, then every 6th row 21 (17, 9, 9, 2, 2) times. Work until the sleeve measures 17" (43 cm), 54 (54, 54, 58, 58, 58) stitches remain, and the pattern has been completed as shown on the chart.

Finishing

Block the garment piece lightly from the wrong side so the texture is not flattened. Pick up and knit *approximately* 128 stitches around the neckline, cable cast-on 3 additional stitches, and then work the I-cord bind off (see page 71). On each sleeve edge, pick up and knit 54 (54, 54, 58, 58, 58) stitches and work I-cord bind-off. Sew the side and sleeve seams. Work in all yarn ends. The lower edge will roll to the right side of the garment.

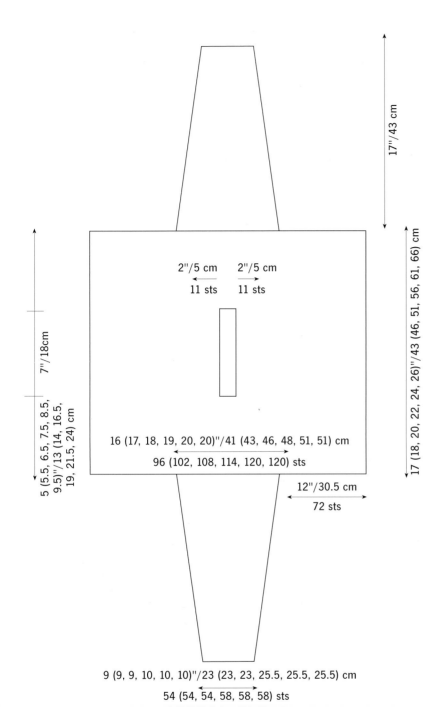

2"/5 cm   2"/5 cm
11 sts   11 sts

17"/43 cm

17 (18, 20, 22, 24, 26)"/43 (46, 51, 56, 61, 66) cm

7"/18cm

5 (5.5, 6.5, 7.5, 8.5, 9.5)"/13 (14, 16.5, 19, 21.5, 24) cm

16 (17, 18, 19, 20, 20)"/41 (43, 46, 48, 51, 51) cm
96 (102, 108, 114, 120, 120) sts

12"/30.5 cm
72 sts

9 (9, 9, 10, 10, 10)"/23 (23, 23, 25.5, 25.5, 25.5) cm
54 (54, 54, 58, 58, 58) sts

Popcorns

These popcorns are knit by making five stitches from one as follows: Purl up to the popcorn base stitch. Knit into the front and the back of this stitch. Make a yarn over to increase and then knit into the front and back again. Drop the old stitch from the left needle. Turn the work over and purl across the 5 popcorn stitches. Turn the work and reduce the 5 stitches back to 1 stitch as follows: slip 1 stitch, *knit 2 together and pass the slipped stitch over.** Repeat from * to **. Please note that on the following row of the chart, the stitch above each popcorn will be worked as a purl stitch as it anchors the popcorns more securely.

Because there are a lot of popcorns in this sweater and because there are so many stitches on the needle, you might want to consider learning to knit backward to minimize turning the work. After a couple of rows, you'll get over the strange new feeling of working stitches off the right needle instead of the left.

Increase from 1 to 5 stitches as described above, but do not turn the work. With the popcorn stitches on the right needle, insert the left needle into the first stitch on the right needle from front to back (under the right needle). (The needle looks exactly the way a right needle would look when you begin to make a purl stitch.) Wrap the yarn from left to right (top to bottom) over the tip of the left needle and then carefully knit the stitch by lifting the right needle up and over the tip of the left needle. (Or, you might find it easier to just back the left needle out of the stitch.) As the old stitch slips off the right needle, the new stitch will be on the left needle.

Shoulder/Neckline

XS, S, M

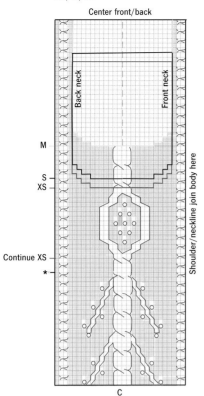

Center front/back

Back neck

Front neck

Shoulder/neckline join body here

M

S

XS

Continue XS

*

C

* Work all sizes to this point.
Sizes S and M continue to
the neckline. For XS, stop at
★ and then continue from
row indicated to neckline.

It's a good idea to make a copy of your
charts so you can check off the rows as
you work. Photocopy them at 150 to
200 percent for easy reference and
greater legibility.

Front/Back

XS, S, M

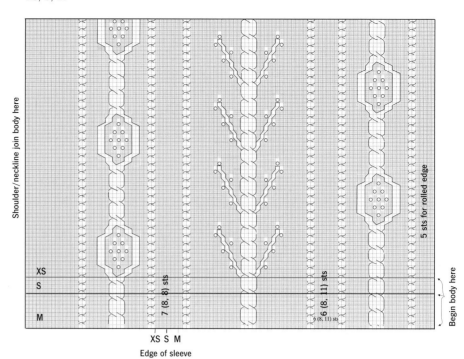

Shoulder/neckline join body here

5 sts for rolled edge

Begin body here

XS

S

M

7 (8, 8) sts

6 (8, 11) sts

9 (8, 11) sts

XS S M

Edge of sleeve

Sleeve

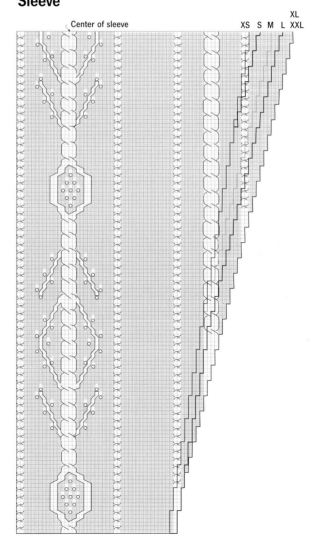

Center of sleeve

XL
XXL
XS S M L

Front/Back

L, XL, XXL

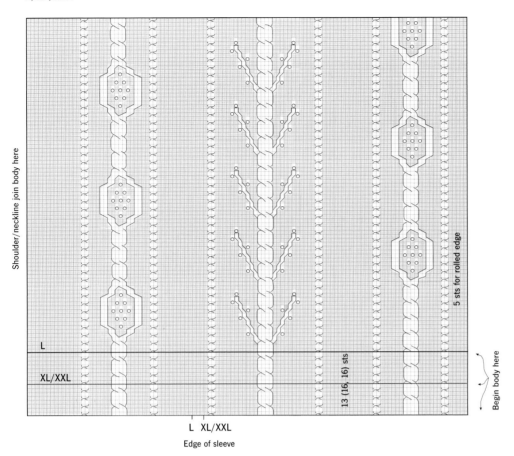

Shoulder/neckline join body here

5 sts for rolled edge

L

XL/XXL

13 (16, 16) sts

Begin body here

L   XL/XXL

Edge of sleeve

Shoulder/Neckline

L, XL, XXL

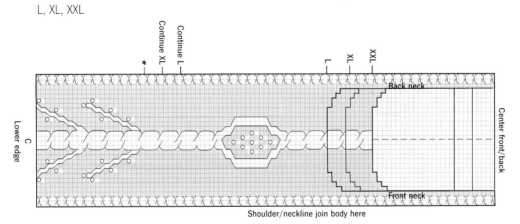

*

Continue XL

Continue L

L

XL

XXL

Back neck

Front neck

Lower edge

C

Center front/back

Shoulder/neckline join body here

*Work all sizes to this point.
For XXL, continue through to
XXL neckline. For L and XL,
stop at * and continue from
the row indicated to the
beginning of the neckline.

fan dancer

This pullover is constructed from two identical pieces and assembled so that the stitch pattern on both sleeves "fans" toward the center of the garment. The pieces are joined with off-center seaming at the front and back, which adds another decorative detail.

Featured Design Variations

- Cropped body with angled extensions at front and back
- Shaped front and back necklines
- I-cord edge knitted onto the garment
- Decorative stitch work in pattern of little alternating "fans"

Yarn: Berroco "Ultra Silk" (20% silk, 40% rayon, 40% nylon with 98 yds/90 meters per 1.75 ounce/50 gram ball), color #6115 Cinnebar, 13 (14, 14, 15, 15, 16) balls

Needles: Size US 10/6 mm OR SIZE TO OBTAIN GAUGE; pair of size US 9/5.5 mm double-pointed needles

Notions: tapestry needle, tape measure, stitch holder, 3 buttons or frog closures (I used JHB #00326.)

Gauge: 21 stitches and 27 rows = 4" (10 cm) in pattern stitch

Sizes: Women's XS (S, M, L, XL, XXL). *Model is wearing size M.*

Finished Measurements:

Garment width: 17 (18, 20, 22, 24, 26)"/43 (46, 51, 56, 61, 66) cm

Garment length at side seam: 18 (18.5, 19, 19, 19.5, 19.5)"/46 (47, 48, 48, 50, 50) cm

Garment length shoulder to lower edge: 22 (22.5, 23, 23, 23.5, 23.5)"/56 (57, 58.5, 58.5, 60, 60) cm

Center back to sleeve edge: 25.5 (26, 27, 28, 29, 30)"/65 (66, 69, 71, 74, 76) cm

See page 17 for detail of stitch pattern

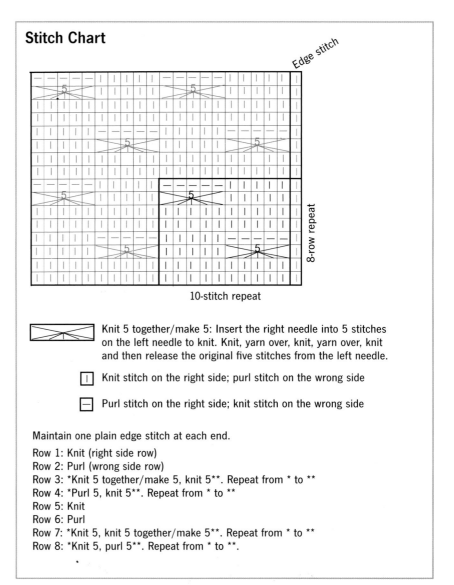

Stitch Chart

Edge stitch

8-row repeat

10-stitch repeat

⊠ Knit 5 together/make 5: Insert the right needle into 5 stitches on the left needle to knit. Knit, yarn over, knit, yarn over, knit and then release the original five stitches from the left needle.

☐ (I) Knit stitch on the right side; purl stitch on the wrong side

☐ (—) Purl stitch on the right side; knit stitch on the wrong side

Maintain one plain edge stitch at each end.
Row 1: Knit (right side row)
Row 2: Purl (wrong side row)
Row 3: *Knit 5 together/make 5, knit 5**. Repeat from * to **
Row 4: *Purl 5, knit 5**. Repeat from * to **
Row 5: Knit
Row 6: Purl
Row 7: *Knit 5, knit 5 together/make 5**. Repeat from * to **
Row 8: *Knit 5, purl 5**. Repeat from * to **.

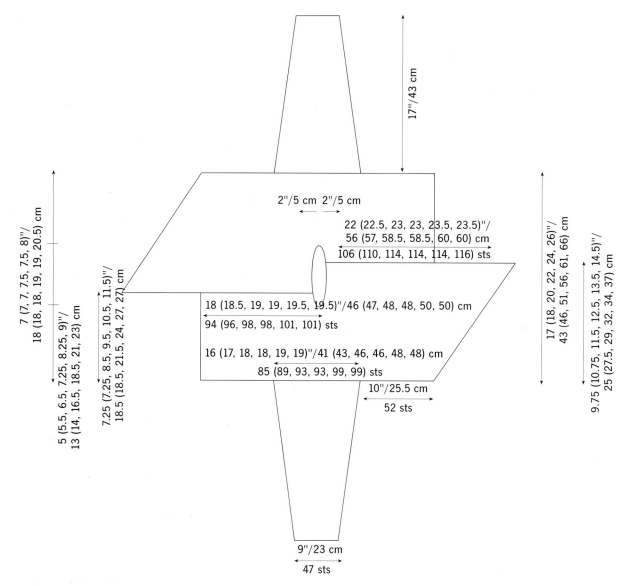

17"/43 cm

2"/5 cm 2"/5 cm

22 (22.5, 23, 23, 23.5, 23.5)"/
56 (57, 58.5, 58.5, 60, 60) cm
106 (110, 114, 114, 114, 116) sts

7 (7, 7, 7.5, 7.5, 8)"/
18 (18, 18, 19, 19, 20.5) cm

7.25 (7.25, 8.5, 9.5, 10.5, 11.5)"/
18.5 (18.5, 21.5, 24, 27, 27) cm

5 (5.5, 6.5, 7.25, 8.25, 9)"/
13 (14, 16.5, 18.5, 21, 23) cm

18 (18.5, 19, 19, 19.5, 19.5)"/46 (47, 48, 48, 50, 50) cm
94 (96, 98, 98, 101, 101) sts

16 (17, 18, 18, 19, 19)"/41 (43, 46, 46, 48, 48) cm
85 (89, 93, 93, 99, 99) sts

10"/25.5 cm
52 sts

17 (18, 20, 22, 24, 26)"/
43 (46, 51, 56, 61, 66) cm

9.75 (10.75, 11.5, 12.5, 13.5, 14.5)"/
25 (27.5, 29, 32, 34, 37) cm

9"/23 cm
47 sts

Insert the right needle into 5 stitches on the left needle as if to knit. Knit, then yarn over (top). Knit, yarn over again. Knit and then complete the stitch by releasing the original 5 stitches from the left needle (bottom).

Step 1

With scrap yarn, cast on 47 stitches (see page 19) and knit a couple of rows. Change to the MC and, following the stitch pattern chart, work 17" (43 cm), *at the same time* increasing 1 stitch each end of every 6th row 18 (14, 10, 10, 4, 4) times and then every 4th row 1 (7, 13, 13, 22, 22) times. Incorporate increased stitches into the stitch pattern, always maintaining 1 plain edge stitch. 85 (89, 93, 93, 99, 99) stitches.

Step 2

At the end of the next 2 rows, cast on/scrap on 52 stitches and work in pattern up to the beginning of the neckline, *at the same time* shape the lower front edge (right end of knitting)

by increasing 1 stitch every 6th row 0 (0, 0, 0, 2, 5) times, then every 4th row 11 (14, 17, 20, 20, 17) times, then every other row 11 (8, 5, 2, 0, 0) times. When the shoulder measures 5 (5.5, 6.5, 7.25, 8.25, 9)"/13 (14, 16.5, 18.5, 21, 23) cm, place 94 (96, 98, 98, 101, 101) stitches for the back onto a stitch holder. Make a note of the pattern row.

Step 3

Working only on the front stitches *and continuing shaping for front extension,* shape the neckline by binding off at the beginning of every alternate row 4 stitches once, 3 stitches once, 2 stitches once, and then 1 stitch twice. When there are 106 (108, 110, 110, 113, 113) stitches on the needle and the extension measures 9.75 (10.75, 11.5, 12.5, 13.5, 14.5)"/25 (27.5, 29, 32, 34, 37) cm, change to scrap yarn, knit a couple of rows, and bind off.

Step 4

Return the back stitches to the needle, continue the pattern from where it ended when the work was divided, and shape the back neckline the same as the front. When the back measures 7.25 (7.25, 8.5, 9.5, 10.5, 11.5)"/18.5, 18.5, 21.5, 24, 27, 29) cm, knit a few rows of scrap and then bind off loosely.

Step 5

Repeat steps 1 to 4 for the second piece.

Finishing

Very lightly block both pieces and press any scrap knitting flat. Sew the side seams. ★With the wrong sides together and the neck edges even, fold back the scrap knitting to combine the stitches and initially join the seam for the two front pieces. (Pick up the first stitch from the shorter piece, the first stitch from the extension piece, and then pass the first stitch over the second.) Repeat until all of the stitches from the shorter piece have been combined with the stitches from the extension piece. There will be 22 more stitches on the extension piece.

Put these stitches on the needle with the combined stitches. Pick up approximately 30 (30, 32, 32, 32, 36) stitches around half of the neckline. Break the yarn. With the right side facing you and beginning at the combined seam, pick up approximately 32 (32, 38, 42, 47, 52) stitches across the straight edge of the lower back, then 44 (48, 52, 56, 60, 65) stitches along the diagonal, ending at the point. Break the yarn. Put all of the picked-up stitches on one long (29" [80 cm]) circular needle. Knit the I-cord edging as described at right. ★★ Repeat from ★ to ★★ for the second half of the garment.

I-Cord Edging

With the right side facing you, and beginning at the edge of the cropped piece, use two double-pointed needles to cast on 3 stitches. *Knit 2, slip 1 (on the double-pointed needles), and then knit 1 stitch from the circular needle. Pass the slipped stitch over the last knit stitch and, with the yarn in back, slide all 3 stitches to the right end of the double-pointed needle.** Repeat from * to **. As you work, the yarn always slips behind the 3 stitches on the double-pointed needle, forming the I-cord as the live stitches on the circular needle are bound off.

Hold the work on your lap so that the weight of the sweater is supported. You will hold the double-pointed needles while you work the I-cord and only intermittently hold the circular needle when you knit the 1 stitch and pass the slipped stitch over it. Working with three needles (the circular needle and a pair of double points) may seem awkward at first, but you will develop a rhythm as the work progresses.

Continue down the angled side of the front extension and then work 3 extra rows on just the I-cord stitches to allow enough extra fabric to turn the corner without puckering. At the neck edge, turn the corner in the same way and continue working the I-cord around to the edge. Cut the yarn and run it back through the 3 remaining stitches to gather them off. Repeat for the second side.

Work the edging around the sleeves by distributing the stitches on 3 of the double-pointed needles, casting the 3 I-cord stitches onto the fourth needle and knitting with the fifth needle as described above.

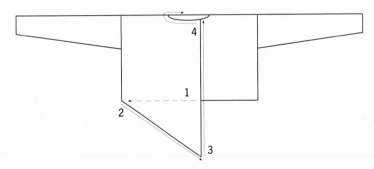

Begin knitting the I-cord trim at the back (1), along the diagonal (2), up the front (3), and around half the neckline (4).

boys' club

Our model is a toddler, but you can knit this sweater—sized from a child's 4 to an adult's XXL—for every member of the family. Because there's no neckline shaping to worry about, this is an easy silhouette to knit, but you will make yarn changes for the stripes.

Featured Design Variations

- Boat neckline
- Turned hems on cuffs and lower edges
- Easy, rolled-edge finish on neckline
- Stitch work is a k6p6 rib

Yarn: Cascade's "Cascade 220" (100% wool worsted with 220 yards/202 meters per 3.5 ounce/100 gram skein), CC1 color #9402 (dark gray/white marl) 1 (1, 2, 2, 2) [2 (2, 3, 3, 4, 4)] skeins; CC2 color #9401 (light white/white marl) 1 (1, 2, 2, 2) [2 (2, 3, 3, 4, 4)] skeins; CC3 color #8400 (white) 1 (1, 1, 2, 2) [2 (2, 3, 3, 3, 3)] skeins; 1 skein each CC4 color #4002 (charcoal), CC5 color #8012 (tan), and CC6 color #7821 (brown)

Needles: Size US 6/4 mm and 8/5 mm needles OR SIZE TO OBTAIN GAUGE; size US 6/4 mm double-pointed needles

Notions: tapestry needle, tape measure, stitch holder

Gauge: 20 stitches and 26 rows = 4" (10 cm) in k6p6 rib

Sizes: Children's 4 (6, 8, 10, 12) [adult XS (S, M, L, XL, XXL)]. *Model is wearing size 4.*

Children's Finished Measurements:

Garment width: 13 (14, 15, 16, 17)"/ 33 (35.5, 38, 41, 43) cm

Garment length: 10.75 (13, 15.5, 15.5, 18)"/27.5 (33, 39.5, 39.5, 46) cm

Center back to cuff: 16.5 (18, 19.5, 21, 22.5)"/42 (46, 50, 53, 57) cm

Adults' Finished Measurements:

Garment width: 18 (20, 22, 24, 26, 27)"/46 (51, 56, 61, 66, 69) cm

Garment length: 20 (20.25, 22.5, 22.5, 24.75, 25)"/51 (51.5, 57, 57, 63, 63.5) cm

Center back to cuff: 27 (28, 29, 30, 31, 31.5)"/69 (71, 74, 76, 79, 80) cm

Notes:

Set up the rib pattern on the first sleeve so that there are 6 knit stitches at the center of the sleeve. This rib will later split to form the neckline. When the body stitches are added later, all sizes should begin (k1, p1) at the lower edge.

When increasing or decreasing sleeves, maintain 2 knit stitches at each edge, whether you are working a knit or purl rib.

Do not slip the first stitch in a row when changing color.

If you want to make the sweater longer or shorter, you must add/subtract stitches in multiples of 12 in order to end up with a knit rib at the lower edge.

Highlight the specifics for your pattern so you are not confused by the multiple-sizing information.

The stripe order is shown in the chart on page 76. This chart tracks the stripes and increases at the same time. Rather than listing every row in the sweater, I just show enough rows to account for the sleeve shaping. I check off each row as I knit and, when I run out of numbered rows on the chart, I go back and double-check the boxes or cross them out.

Stitch Chart

2-edge stitches

Row 2
Row 1

12-stitch repeat

☐ Knit stitch on the right side; purl stitch on the wrong side

☐ Purl stitch on the right side; knit stitch on the wrong side

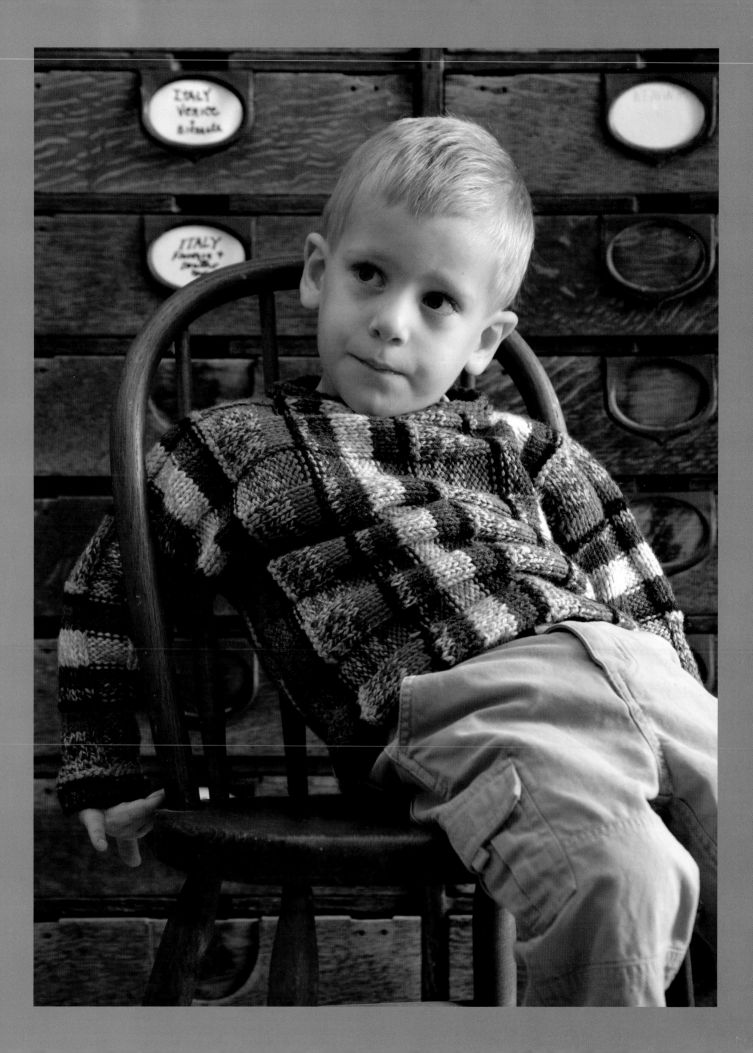

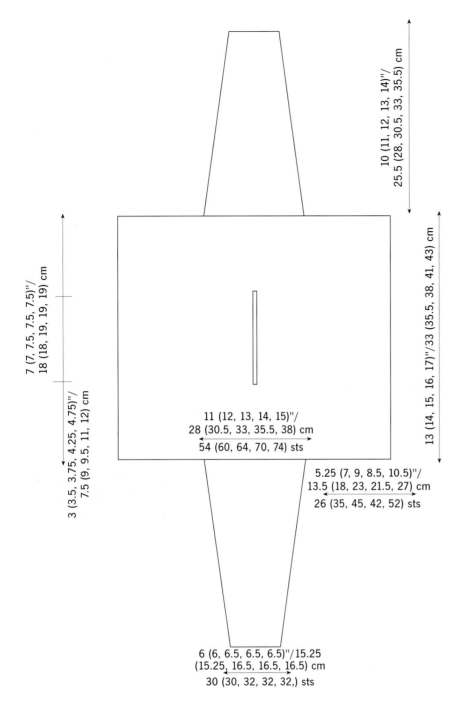

CHILDREN'S SIZING

10 (11, 12, 13, 14)"/
25.5 (28, 30.5, 33, 35.5) cm

7 (7, 7.5, 7.5, 7.5)"/
18 (18, 19, 19, 19) cm

13 (14, 15, 16, 17)"/33 (35.5, 38, 41, 43) cm

11 (12, 13, 14, 15)"/
28 (30.5, 33, 35.5, 38) cm
54 (60, 64, 70, 74) sts

3 (3.5, 3.75, 4.25, 4.75)"/
7.5 (9, 9.5, 11, 12) cm

5.25 (7, 9, 8.5, 10.5)"/
13.5 (18, 23, 21.5, 27) cm
26 (35, 45, 42, 52) sts

6 (6, 6.5, 6.5, 6.5)"/15.25
(15.25, 16.5, 16.5, 16.5) cm
30 (30, 32, 32,) sts

Step 1

With the smaller needles and CC3, loosely cast on 27 (27, 29, 29, 29) [40 (40, 40, 42, 45, 45)] stitches with the simple looped cast-on (see page 90). Knit 6 rows of stockinette, increasing 3 (3, 3, 3, 3) [6 (6, 6, 6, 5, 7)] stitches evenly across the last row. Change to the larger needles and establish the k6p6 ribbing, beginning the first row with knit 6 (6, 7, 7, 7) [2 (2, 2, 3, 4, 5)]. Follow this with purl 6, knit 6, etc., to the end of the row in order to place 6 knit stitches at center of sleeve. Work sleeves, following the stripe pattern shown on page 76, until the sleeve measures 10 (11, 12, 13, 14) [18]"/25.5 (28, 30.5, 33, 35.5) [46] cm from the beginning of the stripe pattern, *at the same time* increasing 1 stitch at each end of every 6th row 8 (5, 7, 4, 3) [16 (12, 6, 4, 4, 2] times then every 4th row 4 (10, 9, 15, 18) [4 (10, 19, 22, 22, 25)] times. 54 (60, 64, 70, 74) [86 (90, 96, 100, 102, 106)] stitches.

Step 2

Cast on/scrap on 26 (35, 45, 42, 52) [58 (56, 65, 63, 74, 72)] stitches at each end of the next row and continue working the stripe pattern across all 106 (130, 154, 154, 178) [202 (202, 226, 226, 250, 250)] stitches. (Double-check that the pattern begins and ends at each lower edge with knit 1, purl 1.) When the right shoulder measures 3 (3.5, 3.75, 4.25, 4.75) [4.5 (5.5, 6, 7, 7.75, 8.25)]"/7.5 (9, 9.5, 11, 12) [11.5 (14, 15.25, 18, 19.5, 21)] cm, work across 53 (65, 77, 77, 89) [101 (101, 113, 113, 125, 125)] stitches and place the remaining 53 (65, 77, 77, 89) [101 (101,

113, 113, 125, 125)] stitches on a holder. (Because you are working with 6 balls of yarn, working both sides at the same time would be unwieldy, so I don't recommend it.)

Step 3

Work the front alone until the neck measures 7 (7, 7.5, 7.5, 7.5) [9 (9, 10, 10, 10.5, 10.5)]"/18 (18, 19, 19, 19) [23 (23, 25.5, 25.5, 27, 27)] cm. Then slip these stitches to a holder and return the back stitches to the needle.

Step 4

Continuing the stripe pattern as before, work the back stitches until the back neckline (and the stripe pattern) matches the front. Then return the front stitches to the needle and work across all 106 (130, 154, 154, 178) [202 (202, 226, 226, 250, 250)] stitches until the left shoulder matches the right shoulder.

Step 5

At the beginning of the next two rows, bind off/scrap off 26 (35, 45, 42, 52) [58 (56, 65, 63, 74, 72)] stitches. Shape the sleeve by decreasing 1 stitch at each end of every 4th row 4 (10, 9, 15, 18) [4 (10, 19, 22, 22, 25)] times and then every 6th row 8 (5, 7, 4, 3) [16 (12, 6, 4, 4, 2] times. 30 (30, 32, 32, 32) [46 (46, 46, 48, 50, 52)] stitches remain and the sleeve measures 10 (11, 12, 13, 14) [18]"/25.5 (28, 30.5, 33, 35.5) [46] cm. Change to the smaller needles and CC3 and evenly decrease 3 (3, 3, 3, 3) [6 (6, 6, 6, 5, 7)] stitches across the next row, knitting all stitches. Work 5 more rows of stockinette and then bind off as loosely as possible.

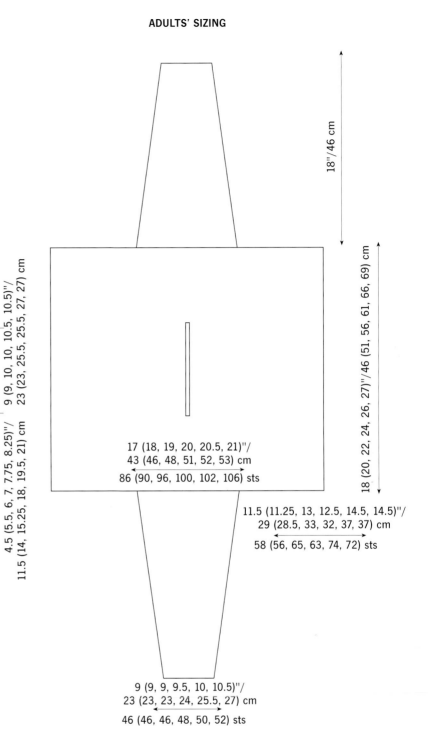

18"/46 cm

18 (20, 22, 24, 26, 27)"/46 (51, 56, 61, 66, 69) cm

9 (9, 10, 10, 10.5, 10.5)"/
23 (23, 25.5, 25.5, 27, 27) cm

4.5 (5.5, 6, 7, 7.75, 8.25)"/
11.5 (14, 15.25, 18, 19.5, 21) cm

17 (18, 19, 20, 20.5, 21)"/
43 (46, 48, 51, 52, 53) cm
86 (90, 96, 100, 102, 106) sts

11.5 (11.25, 13, 12.5, 14.5, 14.5)"/
29 (28.5, 33, 32, 37, 37) cm
58 (56, 65, 63, 74, 72) sts

9 (9, 9, 9.5, 10, 10.5)"/
23 (23, 23, 24, 25.5, 27) cm
46 (46, 46, 48, 50, 52) sts

Stripe Order Chart

The 34-row stripe order repeats throughout the sweater. In order to keep track of the sleeve shaping, I always make a chart like this that shows exactly what color each row should be. I circle or **highlight** the rows where I should increase or decrease.

STRIPE ORDER		KNIT ROWS		
1	CC3	1	35	69
2		2	**36**	70
3		3	37	71
4		**4**	38	72
5	CC4	5	39	73
6		6	**40**	74
7	CC5	7	41	75
8		**8**	42	76
9	CC1	9	43	77
10		10	**44**	78
11		11	45	79
12		**12**	46	80
13		13	47	81
14		14	**48**	82
15		15	49	83
16		**16**	50	84
17	CC6	17	51	85
18		18	**52**	86
19		19	53	87
20		**20**	54	88
21	CC4	21	55	89
22		22	**56**	90
23	CC1	23	57	91
24		**24**	58	92
25	CC3	25	59	93
26		26	**60**	94
27		27	61	95
28		**28**	62	96
29	CC2	29	63	97
30		30	64	98
31		31	65	99
32		**32**	66	100
33		33	67	101
34		34	68	etc.

Finishing

Block the garment to the schematic measurements so that the ribs lie relatively flat and do not contract. Press the sleeve hem facings flat. Sew the side and sleeve seams. With double-pointed needles, CC3, and the right side facing you, pick up *approximately* 80 (80, 86, 86, 86) [104 (104, 115, 115, 122, 122)] stitches around the neck, beginning at one shoulder. Purl 1 round, knit 3 rounds, and bind off loosely.

Turn sleeve hems to the inside and loosely whipstitch in place. With the right side facing, CC3, and the smaller needle, pick up *approximately* 150 (162, 173, 185, 197) [207 (231, 255, 278, 302, 326)] stitches around the lower edge. Knit 6 rounds of stockinette and then bind off loosely. Lightly press the hem, fold it to the inside, and sew in place. Work in all tails.

Hem Finishes

Hems are a great choice for finishing the edges of baby items and Scandinavian-style sweaters and hats. Hems don't interfere with the lines of the sweater, and I often use them when I want a garment that doesn't hug the body. As an alternative to the hem finish on Boys' Club, you can just let the 6 rows of stockinette roll or you can knit a ribbed band for a more fitted look.

The sleeve hems are knitted as part of the sleeves, but you must pick up the lower edge. Lightly press all of the hem facings. Then turn them to the inside and invisibly sew them in place with a strand of the sweater yarn, catching as little as possible of the sweater fabric in each stitch. Space out the stitching so that you catch about 2 to 3 stitches per inch (1 or 2 per centimeter) on the inside of the sweater, which should be secure enough and fairly invisible.

Hems are almost always knitted on needles one or two sizes smaller than the needles used to knit the garment. They are also usually knitted in plain stockinette, regardless of the garment's pattern stitch. To create a sharp crease where the hem folds, work 1 purl row and then finish the hem in stockinette—this single ridge creates a distinct fold line. For a decorative crease, try working one row of eyelets: *Knit 2 together, yarn over**, repeat from * to ** across the row.

Managing the Tails

When you work a six-color stripe, there is no way to avoid having lots of beginning and ending tails. I weave in as many as possible while I knit, which leaves a much more manageable number to hide later.

When I change colors, I do not slip the first stitch in the row. Instead, I knit the first stitch with the new color and then work the next few stitches with the tail and the new yarn, held together as one. This technique keeps the edge stitch from loosening and also gets the tail out of the way so it is less likely to tangle. Yes, the doubled yarn does make those 3 to 4 first stitches a bit bulkier, but the bulk seldom shows. After I assemble the sweater, I just clip the tails. (If you're nervous about their holding, you can always work them through a few more stitches first.)

Whenever possible, I also try to weave old yarn tails through the new working yarn in that first row. Simply cross the old tail over the new yarn before each of the first 5 to 6 stitches, to secure it to the back of the fabric. Unfortunately, this technique only works when you are knitting, not purling. When you are shaping the sleeves, you will at times only have two knit selvage stitches. Secure the tails through these stitches to keep them from loosening while you knit, but when you finish the job, weave them in with a needle or a crochet hook.

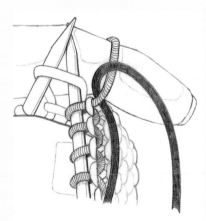

Alternately lay the old tail over your new yarn from right to left, then left to right. The ends should be woven in for about 2" (5 cm) to be sure they are securely bound to the back of the fabric.

luscious

The sleeve seams for this pullover sweater are on top of, rather than under, the arms—so the construction details are a little different than those for the classic cuff-to-cuff sweater.

Featured Design Variations

- Tunic length
- Funnel neck
- Side slits
- Seed stitch edge finishes
- Stockinette body (the knit side is the right side)

Yarn: Classic Elite "Lush" (50% angora rabbit, 50% wool with 123 yards/112 meters per 1.75 ounce/50 gram ball), color #4471, 7 (8, 8, 8, 9, 9) balls

Needles: Size US 7/4.5 mm and US 8/5 mm OR SIZE TO OBTAIN GAUGE; US size 7/4.5 mm double-pointed needles for neck trim (optional)

Notions: tapestry needle, tape measure, 2 stitch holders, stitch markers

Gauge: 18 stitches and 27 rows = 4" (10 cm) in stockinette

Sizes: Women's XS (S, M, L, XL, XXL). *Model is wearing size M.*

Finished Measurements:

Garment width: 17 (18, 20, 22, 24, 26)"/43 (46, 51, 56, 61, 66) cm

Garment length: 21 (21.5, 21.5, 22, 22, 22.5)"/53 (55, 55, 56, 56, 57) cm

Center back to sleeve edge: 25.5 (26, 27, 28, 29, 30)"/65 (66, 69, 71, 74, 76) cm

Stitch Chart

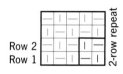

Row 2
Row 1

2-row repeat

⊣ Knit stitch on the right side; purl stitch on the wrong side

— Purl stitch on the right side; knit stitch on the wrong side

Seed stitch is worked (knit 1, purl 1), but unlike ribbing—in which all of the knit and purl stitches line up vertically—the knit and purl stitches alternate from one row to the next.

Notes:

The sleeve, shoulder, and neck are worked with a continuous raised seam on the outside of the garment. The sleeve shaping is worked in increasing or decreasing pairs at the center of the sleeve—rather than at the edges—and the front and the back are knitted separately.

After the first sleeve is knitted, place half of the sleeve stitches on a holder to be worked later with the back of the sweater. The stitches for the front of the garment are cast on next to the remaining sleeve stitches, starting at the center of the sleeve.

When the front is complete, some of the stitches are bound off and others are placed on a holder. Then the back is knitted exactly the same as the front. When both halves are complete, work the sleeve, starting at the shoulder, by picking up the front stitches and then the back stitches so that the sleeve edges fall at the upper arm.

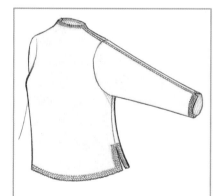

Stitches for the front (or back) are cast on at the center of the sleeve, with the open edge of the sleeve at the shoulder.

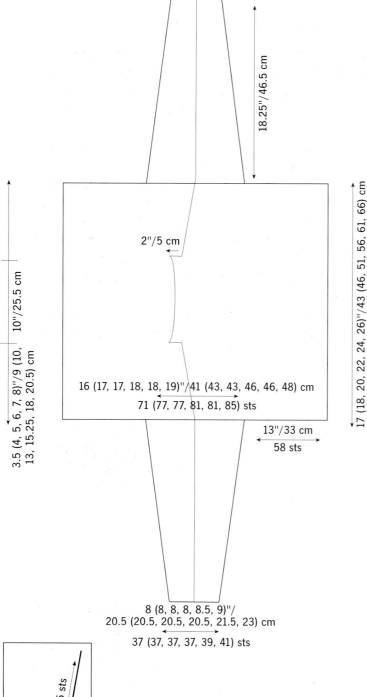

2"/5 cm

16 (17, 17, 18, 18, 19)"/41 (43, 43, 46, 46, 48) cm
71 (77, 77, 81, 81, 85) sts

18.25"/46.5 cm

13"/33 cm
58 sts

17 (18, 20, 22, 24, 26)"/43 (46, 51, 56, 61, 66) cm

10"/25.5 cm

3.5 (4, 5, 6, 7, 8)"/9 (10, 13, 15.25, 18, 20.5) cm

8 (8, 8, 8, 8.5, 9)"/
20.5 (20.5, 20.5, 20.5, 21.5, 23) cm
37 (37, 37, 37, 39, 41) sts

−5 sts

−9 sts

+9 sts

+5 sts

To shape the shoulder slant, increase 1 stitch at the shoulder edge every 10th row 0 (0, 0, 0, 0, 4) times, every 8th row 0 (0, 0, 4, 5, 1) times, every 6th row 0 (3, 5, 1, 0, 0) times, and every 4th row 5 (2, 0, 0, 0, 0) times. Then increase 9 stitches all at once for the funnel neck.

When the neck measures 10" (25.5 cm), bind off 9 stitches all at once and then shape the second shoulder by *decreasing* stitches as listed above.

Step 1

With the smaller needles, cast on 37 (37, 37, 37, 39, 41) stitches and work 6 rows of seed stitch. Place a marker on the center stitch. Change to the larger needles and work in stockinette until the sleeve measures 18.25" (46.5 cm) from the beginning, *at the same time* increase 2 stitches at the center of the sleeve every 8th row 4 (1, 1, 0, 0, 0) times, every 6th row 13 (13, 13, 11, 13, 11) times, and every 4th row 0 (6, 6, 11, 8, 11) times. 71 (77, 77, 81, 81, 85) stitches, ending with a right-side row.

Step 2

Purl across the first 36 (39, 39, 41, 41, 43) stitches, then place the remaining 35 (38, 38, 40, 40, 42) stitches on a holder for the back. Cast on 58 stitches for the front. All rows are worked between the lower edge of the front and the shoulder edge. For the first 4 rows, work the first 58 stitches in seed stitch and the remainder of each row in stockinette. Then work all the following rows in stockinette. *At the same time* increase 1 stitch at the shoulder edge every 10th row 0 (0, 0, 0, 0, 4) times, every 8th row 0 (0, 0, 4, 5, 1) times, every 6th row 0 (3, 5, 1, 0, 0) times, and every 4th row 5 (2, 0, 0, 0, 0) times.

When the front measures 3.5 (4, 5, 6, 7, 8)"/9 (10, 13, 15.25, 18, 20.5) cm from the beginning, cast on 9 stitches at the neck edge and work straight for 10" (25.5 cm), then bind off 9 stitches.

Step 3

Shape the left shoulder by decreasing 1 stitch every 10th row 0 (0, 0, 0, 0, 4) times, every 8th row 0 (0, 0, 4, 5, 1) times, every 6th row 0 (3, 5, 1, 0, 0) times, and every 4th row 5 (2, 0, 0, 0, 0) times. *At the same time,* work the first 58 stitches in seed stitch and the remaining stitches in stockinette for the last 4 rows of the front. Bind off the stitches worked in seed stitch and put the remaining stitches on a holder.

Step 4

Return the second group of sleeve stitches to the needle to work the back exactly like the front.

Step 5

Taking care not to twist the completed sleeve, front, and back, and starting at the shoulder, return the front 36 (39, 39, 41, 41, 43) stitches to the needle. Then, starting at the underarm, return the back 35 (38, 38, 40, 40, 42) stitches to the needle. The second sleeve is worked like the first so that the edges are on top and in line with the shoulder seam.

Work the sleeve for 17.5" (44 cm), *at the same time* decreasing 2 stitches at the center of the sleeve every 4th row 0 (6, 6, 11, 8, 11) times, every 6th row 13 (13, 13, 11, 13, 11) times, and every 8th row 4 (1, 1, 0, 0, 0) times. Change to the smaller needles and work 6 rows of seed stitch. Bind off loosely.

Finishing

Lightly block the garment. With the *wrong* sides together, join both sleeve/shoulder/neck seams with single crochet, working in every other stitch, one full stitch from the edge. Begin working the sleeve seam above the seed stitch border so that there is a small slit at the cuff. Sew the side seams, leaving 5" (13 cm) open from the lower edge.

With double-pointed needles and the right side facing you, pick up approximately 80 stitches around the neck, work 2 rows of seed stitch, then bind off loosely. (The neck edging can also be knitted on a straight needle or back and forth on a longer circular needle after one of the sleeve/shoulder seams is complete.) Pick up approximately 62 (66, 74, 80, 88, 96) stitches from the lower edge of the front, work 6 rows of seed stitch, and bind off loosely. Repeat for the back. Work in all yarn tails.

Paired Increases and Decreases

Shape sleeves with paired increases and decreases at the center of the sleeve, rather than along the edges as usual. Place a marker on the center stitch to make sure the increases or decreases line up vertically. Move the marker as needed as the knitting progresses (the marker is not shown in the drawings).

Make paired increases by making a left increase, knitting 1 stitch, and then making a right increase: Knit up to the marker, insert the left needle into the left loop of the stitch one row down on the right needle, and lift that stitch onto the left needle, as shown in the drawing at top left. Knit the lifted loop and then the marked stitch. Insert the right needle into the right loop of the stitch one row below on the left needle, as shown in the drawing at top right. Lift the loop onto the left needle. Knit the lifted loop and the stitch that was originally above it and then work to the end of the row.

To make paired decreases, knit up to two stitches before the marker. Knit those 2 stitches together, as shown in the drawing at bottom left. Knit the central (marked) stitch, then slip 1, knit 1, and pass the slipped stitch over, as shown in the drawing at bottom right.

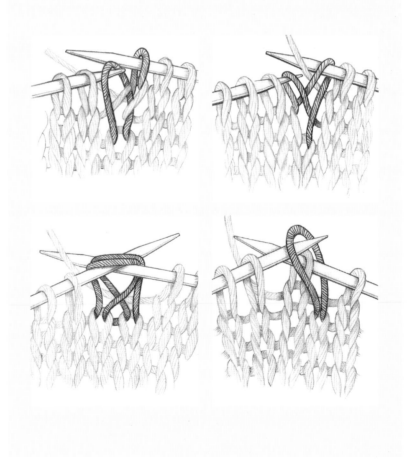

flirt

This feminine, fun sweater—with its deep gores and richly varied colors—moves when you do. The sweater is worked entirely in stockinette stitch and looks terrific whether you wear it on the knit or purl side—you decide!

Featured Design Variations

- Short-rowed gores at lower edge
- Angled neckline
- Simple, single crochet edging

Yarn: Prism "Cool Stuff" (cotton, rayon, nylon, metallic, eyelash with approximately 300 yards/274 meters per 8 ounce/228 gram skein), MC color Periwinkles, 3 skeins; Prism "Quicksilver" (100% rayon with 160 yards/146 meters per 2 ounce/57 gram skein), CC color Wisteria, 1 skein

Needles: Size US 6/4 mm OR SIZE TO OBTAIN GAUGE

Notions: tapestry needle, crochet hook size US E/3.5 mm, tape measure, stitch holder

Gauge: 16 stitches and 24 rows = 4" (10 cm)

Sizes: Women's XS (S, M, L, XL, XXL). *Model is wearing size S.*

Finished Measurements:

Garment width (above gores): 17.25 (18, 20.5, 22.5, 24, 25.5)"/44 (46, 52, 57, 61, 65) cm

Garment width (at lower edge): 25.5 (26, 28.5, 30.5, 32, 33.5)"/65 (66, 72.5, 77.5, 81.5, 85) cm

Garment length: 18 (18, 18.5, 18.5, 19, 19)"/46 (46, 47, 47, 48, 48) cm

Center back to sleeve edge: 25.5 (26, 27, 28, 29, 30)"/65 (66, 69, 71, 74, 76) cm

Notes:

"Cool Stuff" is composed of many very cool yarns knotted together. The knots can be pulled to the wrong side or allowed to show on the right side. It is a matter of personal preference. Some strands are doubled so make sure you catch both strands.

When knitting narrow areas, like sleeves, the yarn repeat may start to look too stripy. To adjust, work with two balls of yarn at the same time, alternately working two rows with each ball. Or cut and reknot the yarn where you would like to change. Save all the pieces you cut off to knot back on later!

You can choose either the knit or the purl side as the right side of this garment—and you don't have to decide until you sew the seams.

Step 1

With MC, cast on 34 (34, 34, 36, 36, 36) stitches and knit until the sleeve measures 17" (43 cm) from the beginning, *at the same time* increasing 1 stitch each end of every 8th row 6 (6, 0, 3, 0, 0) times, every 6th row 9 (9, 17, 13, 15, 14) times, and every 4th row 0 (0, 0, 0, 3, 3) times. 64 (64, 68, 68, 72, 72) stitches.

Step 2

With scrap, cast on 40 stitches at each end of the row (see page 19). Work until the shoulder measures 5 (5.5, 6.5, 7.25, 8.25, 9)"/13 (14, 16.5, 18.5, 21, 23) cm, *at the same time* shaping the gores by short rows (see page 85). There are 5.75 (6, 6.75, 7.5, 8, 8.5)"/14.5 (15.25, 17, 19, 20.5, 21.5) cm between each of the gores. The first gores knitted will be partial, decreased gores, followed by two full gores and a partial, increased gore at the end.

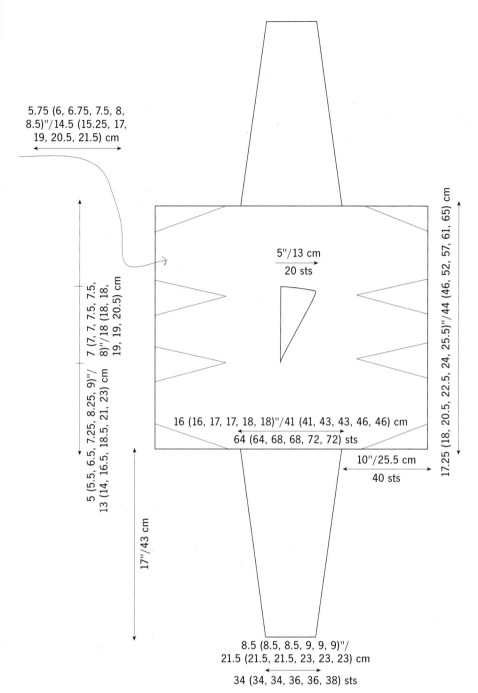

5.75 (6, 6.75, 7.5, 8, 8.5)"/14.5 (15.25, 17, 19, 20.5, 21.5) cm

5"/13 cm
20 sts

7 (7, 7, 7.5, 7.5, 8)"/18 (18, 18, 19, 19, 20.5) cm

5 (5.5, 6.5, 7.25, 8.25, 9)"/13 (14, 16.5, 18.5, 21, 23) cm

17.25 (18, 20.5, 22.5, 24, 25.5)"/44 (46, 52, 57, 61, 65) cm

16 (16, 17, 17, 18, 18)"/41 (41, 43, 43, 46, 46) cm
64 (64, 68, 68, 72, 72) sts

10"/25.5 cm
40 sts

17"/43 cm

8.5 (8.5, 8.5, 9, 9, 9)"/21.5 (21.5, 21.5, 23, 23, 23) cm
34 (34, 34, 36, 36, 38) sts

Step 3

When the first shoulder is complete, put 72 (72, 74, 74, 76, 76) back stitches on a holder and make note of any short-row shaping. Continue working on the remaining 72 (72, 74, 74, 76, 76) stitches for the front. Immediately begin shaping the neck by binding off 4 stitches once, 3 stitches once, 2 stitches once, and 1 stitch 11 times. When the neckline measures 7 (7, 7, 7.5, 7.5, 8)"/18 (18, 18, 19, 19, 20.5) cm, put the front stitches on a holder.

Step 4

Return the back stitches to the needle and continue working gores and plain sections until the back is the same length as the front. Work across the back stitches to the neckline and cast on 20 stitches. Then return the front stitches to the needle and work across all stitches.

Step 5

When the second shoulder matches the first, scrap off 40 stitches at each end of the row and knit the second sleeve for 17" (43 cm), *at the same time* decreasing 1 stitch each end of every 4th row 0 (0, 0, 0, 3, 3) times, every 6th row 9 (9, 17, 13, 15, 14) times, and every 8th row 6 (6, 0, 3, 0, 0) times. Loosely bind off the remaining 34 (34, 34, 36, 36, 36) stitches.

Finishing

Very lightly steam the finished garment. The iron should hover a couple of inches above the surface of the fabric but never rest on it. Graft the side seams and sew the sleeve seams. Work single crochet around the sleeve edges and "knobby" single crochet around neckline and lower edges as follows: ★Work 2 single crochet, then chain 3 stitches. Insert hook in base stitch of chain and draw a loop through the base and then through the stitch on the hook.★★ Repeat from ★ to ★★. Leave tails and knots visible on the right side or work them into the wrong side.

Short-Row Knitting

Short-row knitting, also called partial knitting, is commonly used to add or remove fullness from garments (and to shape shoulders and some necklines) without binding off stitches. Unlike decreasing, which is done at the beginning of a row, short rows are made at the end of rows—but the two techniques are often interchangeable.

To decrease stitches with short-rowing, simply knit across the row until you need to begin to decrease. Bring the yarn to the front as if to purl, slip the first stitch from the left needle to the right, put the yarn in back, and then return the stitch to the left needle. The yarn now encircles, or wraps, the first stitch on the left needle—which prevents a hole from forming when you turn the work and knit back to the starting edge. If you later knit across all the stitches (or seam a short-rowed edge), be sure to insert the right needle into both the wrap and the stitch it encircles and treat them as one stitch.

To wrap when working short rows from the purl side, bring the yarn to the back, slip the first stitch, and then bring the yarn to the front again before returning the stitch to the left needle.

Unless you wrap partial rows, there will be a hole when the work is turned. If knitting, bring the yarn to the front (as if to purl), and if purling, bring the yarn to the back (as if to knit). Then slip 1 stitch from the left needle to the right, put the yarn back to where it was, and return the slipped stitch to the left needle.

Knitting the Gores

There are two complete gores and two partial gores on the front and the back of Flirt. The first partial gores are knitted as decrease gores. The partial gores at the other end of the body are worked as increase gores.

Complete an entire gore on one side of the garment before working across the fabric to knit the corresponding gore on the other side. When knitting the front and back at the same time for the shoulders, complete a front gore, then work one row across the full width of the sweater to work the corresponding back gore, as shown in the diagram.

To increase each gore with short rows: Knit 8 stitches, wrap, turn, and purl back. Then knit 16, wrap, turn, and purl back. On subsequent alternate rows, knit 24, then 32 stitches before turning and purling back. You will have knitted 8 (short) rows.

To decrease each gore with short rows: Knit 24 stitches, wrap, turn, and purl back. Then knit 8 fewer stitches every alternate row until none of the stitches is a knit stitch. You will have knitted 6 (short) rows.

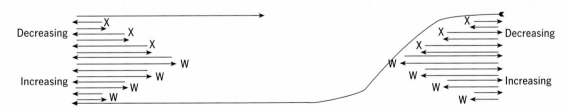

W = Wrap, turn, and knit back.
X = Knit the wrap and the stitch it encircles when working the subsequent row.

Knitting by Machine

Some of you might also be machine knitters (or aspire to be), so here are some pointers in case you'd like to machine-knit any of the twelve sweaters in this book. You may have your own methods, so don't feel that you have to do things exactly as I am suggesting. Also, depending on your machine's gauge, you might have to use a different yarn than the one listed for the hand-knit sweater.

Not every sweater can be knitted on every type of machine—and not every sweater can be knitted exactly like the hand-knit version. Except for the smallest sizes, none of these sweaters can be made in one piece because most machines simply don't have enough needles to accommodate all the stitches. Generally, standard-gauge machines have 200 needles, mid-gauge have 150, and chunky/bulky machines have 110, with minor variations from one brand to another. Each of these machines handles a very specific range of yarns. The Boys' Club sweater (page 72) requires a ribber, but you could knit it on a single-bed machine with hand-latched ribs.

The hand-knit stitch counts are the same for machine knitting, but all measurements must be converted to row counts. Knit a couple of gauge swatches to get as close as you can to the row gauge of the pattern. If you can't match the gauge you will need to rechart. I can almost always match hand-knit gauges if I am persistent. Try the clicks between full-stitch sizes and adjust the tension mast. Of course, if you have a charting attachment, you just need to draw the schematic onto a sheet of scaled paper and use the stitch ruler that matches your gauge. You may also be able to rework the pattern with a computer charting program.

Work all increases and decreases one stitch from the edge to facilitate seaming and finishing. I usually prefer full-fashioned shaping, and it's up to you whether to use a 2-prong or 3-prong tool. Luscious (page 78) is easiest to shape with a garter bar or multipronged transfer tool because the shaping is done at the center of the sleeve, and you need to move lots of stitches for each increase/decrease.

Consult your knitting machine manual for any operating instructions specific to your machine. For stitch patterning and techniques, my first book, *Hand-Manipulated Stitches for Machine Knitters* (Taunton Press, 1990), is full of ideas and information. (The book is currently out of print, but you can probably locate a copy through your local library or online.)

Step 1:
Knitting the Right Sleeve
Cast on the number of stitches required for the right sleeve, then knit the sleeve, increasing as the pattern specifies for your size. Unless you are working a ribbed band with a ribber bed (or double-bed machine), start with scrap knitting and pick up the edge later on.

Step 2:
Knitting to the Neckline
When you finish knitting the first sleeve, you need to cast on additional stitches on either side of the sleeve to create the fabric that will make up the front and back sections

Machine Recommendations

M = mid-gauge
B = bulky
C = chunky
S = standard
EONS = every other needle
         standard gauge

Note: Although many yarns will knit on every other needle of a standard-gauge machine, you will only have 100 needles to work with.

of the garment. If your machine has enough needles to accommodate both the back and the front of the garment in the size you are knitting, follow the directions for the hand-knit version. To divide the neckline, however, instead of putting the unused stitches on a holder, simply put the needles into holding position.

Most machines are just not wide enough to accommodate all the garment stitches, however, and so at this point the machine-knit directions vary from the hand-knit directions. Tag the center sleeve stitch and scrap off the entire sleeve. Determine the number of needles you will need for half of the sleeve stitches and the front body stitches and plan their placement on the bed. I find it easiest to begin the body stitches at center zero, but you can't always do this, depending on the garment size.

Scrap on the required number of stitches for the body on the left of the bed and then, with the wrong side facing you, rehang half of the sleeve stitches next to them. Make sure the *edge* stitch of the sleeve, not the center stitch, abuts the body stitches. Knit the required number of rows for the shoulder.

Step 3:
Shaping the Front Neckline

Shape the front neckline according to the pattern instructions—usually by decreasing stitches at the right edge of the neckline, working several inches without further shaping, then increasing stitches for the left side of the neckline. Some necklines can be shaped with short rows. After you shape the neckline, knit the left shoulder to match the right and then scrap off the front.

Step 4:
Knitting the Back

Knit the back by scrapping on the body stitches on the right side of the bed and rehanging the second half of the sleeve stitches. Knit the entire back, starting with right shoulder, neckline shaping, and left shoulder. Then scrap off the back.

Step 5:
Knitting the Left Sleeve

With the wrong side facing you, rehang an equal number of stitches from the back and front of the sweater to equal the number of stitches required for the top of the sleeve. It's easier to keep track of decreases if you center the sleeve on the bed. Knit the sleeve, decreasing as specified in the pattern, and then scrap off the remaining stitches.

Crayon Stripes
Page 28
Machine: M, B, EONS
Patterning: Stockinette

Weekend Woodsman
Page 32
Machine: M, B, EONS
Patterning: Re-form alternate groups of 3 stitches with a latch tool every other row.

Chiquita Jacketta
Page 36

Machine: As needed for substituted yarn and gauge

Patterning: To machine-knit this sweater, you need to rechart it with a lighter-weight yarn. The basic shaping can easily be adapted to any of the other sweater patterns because there is virtually no neck shaping.

Summer Twist
Page 42

Machine: M, S, or EONS

Patterning: Twisted stitches are easily made as follows: Remove a pair of stitches on a 2-prong transfer tool. Rotate the tool 180 degrees to the right and slip another 2-prong tool into the same stitches. Remove the first tool and then replace the stitches on the needles. You can also use a pair of single-prong transfer tools and treat them as 1 x 1 cables—but there are a lot of stitches and this method would be much slower. Work the garter stitch bands by hand.

Jewels
Page 46

Machine: M, B, C

Patterning: This sweater must be worked in something other than garter stitch, which requires turning the work over after every row. Swatch some tuck or slip stitches to create interesting textures and rechart accordingly, as the row gauge will definitely not match. Make sure you position the body stitches on the machine to allow for the increasing length of the front ties.

Classic Stripes
Page 50

Machine: M, B, EONS

Patterning: This sweater must be worked in something other than garter stitch, which requires turning the work over after every row. Swatch some tuck or slip stitches to create interesting textures and rechart accordingly, as the row gauge will definitely not match. The edges will require a row of crochet to prevent them from rolling.

Autumn Leaves
Page 56

Machine: M, B, C

Patterning: To work the wrapped stitch manually, hold all the stitches except the "bridge" up to the first pair of pattern stitches and the two pattern stitches themselves. ★Knit across the bridge/pattern stitches, remove the last two stitches just knitted with a transfer tool, then wrap the yarn around these stitches twice using the "free yarn" between the carriage and the bed. Place all the stitches just knitted and wrapped into holding position. Return the next bridge and pair of pattern stitches to working position★★ and repeat from ★ to ★★. This is not an exact replication of the hand-knit stitch, but close enough. You could also instead simply substitute slip stitch patterning for the wrapped stitch.

Corn and Cables
Page 62
Machine: M, S

Patterning: This is a complex project—by hand or machine—but all of the texture stitches can be replicated manually. You'll need to consult *Hand-Manipulated Stitches for Machine Knitters* or other sources for detailed instructions. The I-cord edging can be knitted and attached on the machine, but make sure you properly support the weight of the sweater while you work.

Boys' Club
Page 72
Machine: M, B, EONS

Patterning: You can work the 6 x 6 rib with a ribber/double-bed machine or latch it up by hand. For the hem, pick up the lower edge before both side seams have been sewn. Reduce the stitch size for the inside of the hem by at least one full-stitch size. All knitting machine manuals provide detailed information about making hems.

Flirt
Page 82
Machine: M, B, C

Patterning: Follow the instructions in your knitting machine manual for short-row, or partial, knitting. Although this garment's yarn will knit on the machine, keep a keen eye on the knots as they pass through the tension unit. Knit much more slowly than usual to accommodate the different textures and yarn sizes.

Fan Dancer
Page 68
Machine: M, B

Patterning: To replace the fan stitch, swatch some tuck or slip stitches to create interesting textures and rechart accordingly. The I-cord edging can be knitted and attached on the machine, but make sure you properly support the weight of the sweater while you work.

Luscious
Page 78
Machine: M, B, EONS

Patterning: You need to work the seed stitch detail by hand. When rehanging sleeves, the center of the sleeve abuts the body stitches, rather than the sleeve edges. Make sleeve increases and decreases with a garter bar or with multiple moves of a multipronged transfer tool.

Glossary of Basic Techniques

Here are some of the basic techniques you'll need when working through the patterns in this book. I have also included some recommendations as to which techniques work best for particular sweaters. New knitters may find this glossary especially helpful. If you are a more experienced knitter, refer to it as needed.

Casting On and Binding Off

Most knitters have their favorite cast-on and bind-off methods. Unless your pattern specifies a particular method—to accommodate a specific yarn, technique, or finishing method—you can usually choose whichever you prefer. Here are some of the standards:

The simple looped cast-on is fast and easy, but unsuitable for starting conventional or cuff-to-cuff sweaters. This cast-on produces a slack, somewhat sloppy edge, which works just fine on swatches. You can also use it when casting on the body stitches after you have knit the first sleeve because those edges

Simply wrap your finger with loops that resemble the lowercase letter "e" and then slip the loops onto the needle.

are going to be seamed. The looped cast-on is one of the least bulky cast-ons, so it creates a less noticeable, less bulky seam. To form a looped cast-on, simply twist little e-shaped wraps around your right index finger and then slip each one onto the needle.

The long-tail cast-on is quick and produces a nice, firm edge for your knitting. Be careful not to tighten each stitch too much. If you do, the first row will be difficult to knit

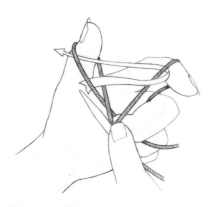

After each stitch is formed, you will have to reposition the "heart" on your left hand to make the next stitch. The process becomes faster and more automatic with each stitch.

and the edge may be too firm or draw in the knitting. The long-tail cast-on is a good, all-purpose cast-on, although it's not a practical way to add body stitches.

To make a long-tail cast-on, pull out twice as much length as you think you'll need and make a slip

knot around the needle. Hold both the long tail and the continuous yarn in the palm of your left hand. (I usually pinch the yarns with my little finger and my ring finger to create some tension.) Insert your thumb and index finger between the two yarns and move them away from each other so that the strands create a heart shape. ★Scoop the tip of the needle under the left strand of the left side of the heart (from left to right) and then over the left strand of the right side of the heart, pulling it through from right to left. Snug the stitch on the needle ★★ and repeat from ★ to ★★.

The cable cast-on is another good, all-purpose cast-on. It works well for adding the side body stitches, increasing the second side of a neckline, making one-row buttonholes, and increasing the tabs at the bottom of the children's Classic Stripes sweater (page 50).

Make a slip knot on the left needle and knit it as a stitch, then place this new stitch on the left needle. ★Insert the right needle in the space behind the first stitch on the left needle and knit it as a stitch. Instead of dropping the stitch from

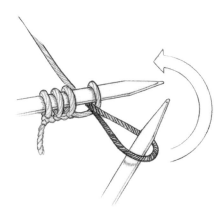

When slipping the new stitches onto the needle, be consistent in how you do or don't twist them so that the edge is uniform.

the left needle or moving stitches to the right needle, the new loop is slipped onto the left needle.★★ Repeat from ★ to ★★ until enough stitches have been cast on. To keep the stitches from tightening too much, I insert my right needle into the space for the next stitch before tightening the previous one.

The most basic bind-off is all you'll need for the sweaters in this book. Slip the first stitch, knit the next stitch, and then pass the slipped

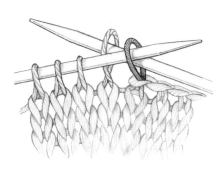

The key to this bind-off is to knit the stitches looser than usual, making sure they do not tighten as you pass over each slipped stitch.

stitch over the knit stitch. Continue knitting one more stitch and passing the previous stitch over it until there is one stitch left or until you have bound off enough stitches and want to continue knitting on the remaining stitches. When binding off all of the stitches, simply cut the yarn and pull it through the last stitch.

The three-needle bind-off is used to join two sets of live stitches in a seam. The effect is much less bulky than it would be if you bound off both sets of stitches and then seamed them. Each set of stitches remains on a needle. (I will sometimes work this

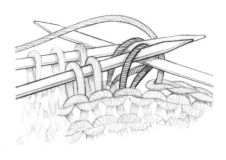

If you find it difficult to draw the yarn through two sets of stitches, try substituting a crochet hook for the third needle.

bind-off on stitches that I have scrapped off, first feeding them back onto needles.)

Hold the two needles in your left hand, with the right sides of the fabric together, and work a basic bind-off with a third needle. The only difference between the three-needle bind-off and the basic bind-off is that you insert the right needle through *two* stitches

each time, one on each of the two left needles.

I-Cords

I-cords are versatile tubes that can be knitted on as few as 2 stitches, but usually on 3 or 4. They represent circular knitting at its smallest! I-cords make good ties, belts, and trimmings of all kinds. They can also be used as a bind-off method (see Fan Dancer, page 68). Two-stitch I-cords look square, 3- to 5-stitch cords look like round shoelaces, and wider cords begin to flatten.

You work I-cords on two, short, double-pointed needles. Cast on 3 stitches and knit 1 row. Do not turn the work over. ★Slide the knitting back to the beginning of the row, letting the yarn float across the back of the stitches and knit 1 row. Do not turn.★★ Repeat from ★ to ★★ for the desired length. When you give the finished tube a good tug, the stitches realign themselves and absorb the little gaps created as you carry the yarn across the back of the stitches to begin each row.

Increasing and Decreasing

There are many ways to increase and decrease—and you really don't need to know them all. If you have methods you prefer, please use them. When practical, I like to pair my increases and decreases so that they slant in opposite directions at each edge of a sleeve or neckline. To ensure an even edge—and perfect seams—remember to work increases and decreases one stitch from the edge of the fabric.

The following methods are for increasing or decreasing knit stitches on the right side of the fabric, but you can also work them on the purl side—simply substitute the word "purl" for "knit" in the directions.

Paired Increases

Left slanting increase: Knit 1 stitch, then insert the left needle into the left loop of the stitch two rows below the stitch just knitted. Knit this loop as a stitch (or lift the loop onto the needle and then knit it). This increase will slant to the left.

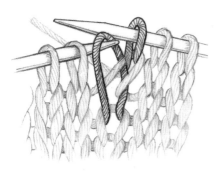

You may find it easier to knit the loop two rows below by lifting it onto the left needle first.

Right slanting increase: Insert the right needle into the right loop of the stitch one row below the next stitch on the left needle, then knit this loop (or lift the loop onto the needle and then knit it) and the original stitch above it. This increase slants towards the right.

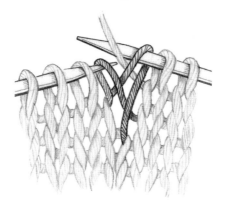

The loop one row below is knitted before the stitch above it.

Paired Decreases

The SKP decrease slants towards the left. Slip 1 stitch, knit 1 stitch, then pass the slipped stitch over the knit stitch.

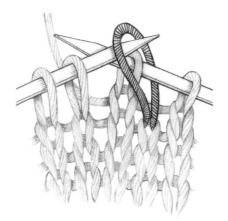

The slipped stitch should be slipped as if to knit.

The K2tog decrease slants towards the right. Insert the right needle into 2 stitches on the left needle and knit the 2 stitches together.

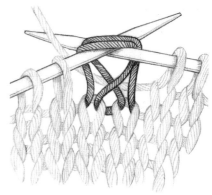

On the purl side of the fabric, this decrease is worked as purl 2 together.

Sources of Supply

Berroco, Inc.
14 Elmdale Road
Box 367
Uxbridge, MA 01569 USA
phone: (508) 278-2527
email: info@berroco.com
www.berroco.com

Cascade Yarns
www.cascadeyarns.com

Classic Elite Yarns, Inc.
122 Western Avenue
Lowell, MA 01851 USA
phone: (978) 453-2837
www.classiceliteyarns.com

Colinette Yarns
distributed in the United States by
Unique Kolours
28 N. Bacton Hill Road
Malvern, PA 19355 USA
phone: (610) 644-4885
toll-free phone: (800) 25-2DYE4;
(800) 252-3934
www.uniquekolours.com

Design Source
(Manos del Uruguay Yarns)
toll-free phone: (888) 566-9970
email: shangold@aol.com

JHB International, Inc.
1955 South Quince Street
Denver, CO 80231 USA
phone: (303) 751-8100
email: sales@buttons.com
www.buttons.com

Knitting Fever, Inc.
PO Box 336
Amityville, NY 11701 USA
phone: (516) 546-3600
toll-free phone: (800) 645-3457
email: knittingfever@
    knittingfever.com
www.knittingfever.com

Mountain Colors Yarn
PO Box 156
Corvallis, MT 59828 USA
phone: (406) 961-1900
email: info@mountaincolors.com
www.mountaincolors.com

Prism Arts, Inc.
3140 39th Avenue North
St. Petersburg, FL 33714 USA
phone: (727) 528-3800
email: info@prismyarn.com
www.prismyarn.com

Simply Shetland (Jamieson's)
10 Domingo Road
Santa Fe, NM 87508 USA
www.simplyshetland.net

Skacel Collection, Inc.
(Addi Turbo Cro-Needle)
PO Box 88110
Seattle, WA 98138 USA
phone: (425) 291-9600
email: info@skacelknitting.com
www.skacelknitting.com

Tahki/Stacy Charles, Inc.
70-30 80th Street, Building 36
Ridgewood, NY 11385 USA
phone: (800) 338-YARN;
(800) 338-9276
www.tahkistacycharles.com

Meet the Knitters

I'm fortunate to have some wonderful friends—and doubly lucky that so many of them are great knitters! I designed all of the sweaters in this book, but I knitted only two of them. The other ten were knitted by friends who are scattered all around the country. Knitters are usually the unsung heroes of most magazines and books, but I'd like to introduce you to my cadre of hand-knitting experts!

Margaret Bruzelius
Northampton, Massachusetts

Margaret usually hires people to knit *her* sweater designs, so I was honored when she agreed to knit the short-rowed sweater Flirt (page 82). Margaret's work has been featured in many top knitting magazines. She is also a dean at Smith College in Northampton, Massachusetts. I knew Margaret by reputation, and when my sister-in-law and I opened a yarn shop in Cheshire, Connecticut, we discovered we lived in the same town. I always feel energized after spending time with Margaret!

Laurencia Ciprus
Essex, Connecticut

I met Laurencia while I was working as the education director for a handcraft center in Guilford, Connecticut. She was one of the loyal volunteers who made the place tick! Coincidentally, her mother, who I knew only as "Sweater Rescue," was the woman who did all of the knitting repair work for the yarn shop I ran for several years. Laurencia is a fast knitter, and I knew she'd come through for me! She added the chart that clarifies the "slides" for Jewels (page 46).

Jeanne Drury
Hamden, Connecticut

Jeanne was a customer at my shop, Have You Any Wool?, and eventually started teaching classes for us. She loves color work and cables and has the patience of a knitting saint, which is why she is such an excellent teacher. An architect by day, Jeanne has a keen understanding of details and was actually able to work from my initial, rough sketches and charts to knit Corn and Cables (page 62). She had the great idea to knit the popcorns backward to streamline the process.

Carol Marcarelli
North Haven, Connecticut

Carol is my sister-in-law and dear friend and also my former partner in the yarn shop in Cheshire, Connecticut. She knits constantly, and I designed Classic Stripes (page 50) for one of her granddaughters. Carol is an experienced knitter and an excellent teacher. She even taught her husband how to knit one winter when they were snowed in week after week!

Lynne McClune
East Sound, Washington

Lynne was a knitting educator when I worked for Studio by White Knitting Machines. She was one of the few machine knitters I knew who also knit by hand—and made it look just as fast and easy! When Lynne left Studio, she took on the job of coordinating the huge Stitches shows for *Knitters* magazine for several years. She and I both look best in blue-reds, which is the color of the yarn I chose for Fan Dancer (page 68).

Brenda O'Brien
Wallingford, Connecticut

Brenda was one of my customers at the yarn shop and later an employee. A fast and excellent hand-knitter, she took to the machines immediately, which made her a great asset to the store. She's also one of the most positive people I know. Brenda hand-knitted Weekend Woodsman (page 32) twice—because of a yarn change—and still got it done in time!

Kate Perri

White Plains, New York

Kate "picked me up" in the grocery store about 30 years ago. I was carrying a hand-woven shoulder bag that gave me away as a "fiber person." She spotted it right away. The next day, she came to visit my weaving studio, and we've been friends ever since. Kate is a quilter and sewer who knits on the side. Chiquita Jacketta (page 36) was a quick project that she fit in between her many commitments.

Toni Salerno

Redondo Beach, California

Toni was one of my weaving students (my then-three-year-old son kicked her in the shins the first time she came to class). Later, she became one of my machine-knitting students. We live on opposite coasts but manage to stay in touch and see each other from time to time, packing more activity into a four-day visit than anyone I know! The book wouldn't have been complete without Toni and Autumn Leaves (page 56), knit in the vibrant, earthy colors I always associate with her.

Lisa Wolkow

Madison, Connecticut

Lisa is one of those people who easily makes me laugh. Working with her was one of the best things about working at Guilford Craft Center. She is a brilliant ceramic artist and also one of the fastest, most even hand-knitters I have ever met. Lisa used to knit sample sweaters for some big-name fashion designers, so I was delighted when she agreed to knit Crayon Stripes (page 28) for me.

Gini Woodward

Bonners Ferry, Idaho

Gini is a well-known machine knitter and teacher. We became friends during my Studio by White days, and despite the fact that there is a whole country between us, we have remained close, constant friends. If we lived any closer to each other, we would be exhausted! Both a hand and machine knitter, Gini understands knits in the same way that I do. I can always rely on her for good advice and feedback. She knitted Summer Twist (page 42).

About the Author

Designer Susan Guagliumi has created original handknit and machine-knit garments for *Vogue Knitting, Knitters,* and *Family Circle Easy Knitting.* She is also the author of *Hand Manipulated Stitches for Machine Knitters* (Taunton Press, 1990) and has written numerous articles for *Handmade, Threads,* and other craft and fiber magazines. Susan wrote and appeared in a series of instructional videos for Studio by White Knitting Machines. She lives in Northford, Connecticut, with her husband, Arthur.

Credits

Without beautiful yarns, knitting would be no fun at all. Sincere thanks to Berroco, Inc.; Cascade Yarns; Classic Elite Yarns, Inc.; Design Source; KFI; Mountain Colors; Prism Arts, Inc.; Simply Shetland; Tahki/Stacy Charles, Inc.; and Unique Kolours for supplying gorgeous yarns, and to JHB Buttons for the finishing touches. Special thanks to Norah Gaughan, Jim Baldini, Linda Pratt, and Andra Asars.